SOCIALISM AND FREEDOM

SOCIALISM AND FREEDOM

Bryan Gould

MACMILLAN

First published 1985

Published by
THE MACMILLAN PRESS LTD
Houndmills, Basingstoke, Hampshire RG21 2XS
and London
Companies and representatives
throughout the world

Typeset by
Wessex Typesetters
Frome, Somerset

Printed and bound in Great Britain by
Anchor Brendon Ltd, Tiptree, Essex

British Library Cataloguing in Publication Data
Gould, Bryan
Socialism and freedom.
1. Liberty   2. Socialism
I. Title
323.44   JC585
ISBN 0–333–40580–3
ISBN 0–333–40581–1 Pbk

Contents

v

Preface

This book is concerned with a specific issue – the compatibility of socialism with individual liberty. It does not, and is not intended to, provide a comprehensive treatment of the many other questions which a modern socialist might find interesting and important, although some of these do arise, and are discussed, as incidentals to the main theme.

Much of today's political discussion on the left is bedevilled by what I call 'politics by label'; ideas are assessed according to the labels – (left-wing, right-wing, and so on) – which can be attached to them, rather than according to their substance or merits. This seems to me to be a fatal inhibition to rational discussion.

The ideas advanced here are not, I hope and believe, easily labelled in this way. With their emphasis on the individual, they will seem to some socialists – superficially at least – to come from the right; but their underlying egalitarianism makes them a good deal more radical than much of what is currently claimed to be left-wing.

I refer, in many passages, to 'the individual', 'the citizen' and so on. These expressions are neutral in terms of gender; when they are represented by pronouns, the use of the masculine form reflects the limitations and conventions of the language, rather than any sexist blind spot on my part.

I am grateful to the members of the Socialist Philosophy Group, and particularly to David Miller, Raymond Plant and Julian Le Grand, for suggestions and encouragement. Michael Hinton, Peter George, Roger Elbourne and David Perrin also helped to point me in useful directions.

B.G.

1   Introduction

SOCIALISM TODAY

The Labour Party in Britain is not and never has been an exclusively socialist Party. It is nevertheless the only practical instrument available to carry into government the ideas and ideals of socialism; Labour's defeat in the 1983 general election must therefore be regarded not only as a Party defeat but as a setback for British socialism.

The nature and scale of that defeat meant that it was more than a purely electoral reverse. It marked, confirmed and gave further impetus to a sea-change in the battle of ideas. The deliberately ideological nature of the successful campaign by the Party's right-wing opponents, the arrival on the scene of a non-socialist alternative to Labour and the paucity of the Labour Party's own intellectual position all pointed to a peculiarly decisive outcome, and one which left the Labour Party, and British socialism, in a parlous condition.

For the best part of this century, the advance of socialist ideas had seemed inevitable. Reactions against the excesses of capitalism and *laissez-faire* liberalism, the social upheaval caused by war, the sense of progress engendered by technological advance and rising living standards, all contributed to a welcome for the idea that we should strive for and could achieve a way of organising society which was at the same time more rational and more compassionate.

Perhaps most importantly, there was a feeling that the tide of history was taking us towards socialism; even those who railed against it conceded the virtual futility of resistance. Partly under the influence of Marxist predictions about the evolutionary nature of the advance to socialism, partly as the result of empirical observation of socialist ideas becoming established in many countries round the world, it was assumed, particularly by the British Labour party, that the victory of socialism was

1

inevitable – and that Fabian gradualism would inexorably produce the socialist millenium.

Many of these assumptions have been falsified by recent experience and in many cases by changes to which the Labour Party has itself contributed. The Labour Party was firmly based on class interest rather than ideology; when working people got the vote and were able to organise industrially they created the Labour Party as their instrument for the exercise of political and Parliamentary power. As long as the working class retained its identity and its numerical importance, the Labour Party – and the socialist ideas of its leaders, if not of its supporters – seemed immune from changing political fashion.

But the old working class, in terms of both numbers and its sense of identity, has been eroded, not least by the social, educational and economic advances which the Labour Party itself has made possible. The class base of the Labour Party is no longer enough to sustain it in power. To achieve majority support, the Party must look beyond its class base and make a deliberate appeal to those whose loyalty has to be won rather than simply assumed.

The demise of capitalism no longer seems quite so inevitable. Capitalism has reformed itself and performed better than its detractors predicted. As more and more people have operated successfully in a capitalist or at least a mixed economy, they have become partisans of private property and of taking one's chance in the market. They have looked more critically at, and demanded more from, socialist reforms and institutions.

Moreover, the sort of society towards which Fabian gradualism has been taking us has now assumed firmer contours. People are not sure that they like what they see. Socialism in action has been seen to have minuses as well as pluses. More importantly, socialism in other countries has increasingly provided a model of what to avoid rather than emulate.

And, in the last decade, when economic growth no longer seems the easy trick it once was, socialism has come to seem, paradoxically, less relevant. This is because it had been sold in Britain as a conscience-salving and painless extra which could easily be afforded among the other fruits of increased affluence; when the affluence is no longer guaranteed, socialism – or a social conscience – is one of the first of life's little luxuries to be dispensed with.

For all these reasons, the will to resist socialism has grown. But the most significant breakthrough has come with the realisation that resistance is possible, that the socialist advance can be stopped. This has been, in Britain at least, the most far-reaching change. It has been helped by, and has in turn given succour to, a tremendous revival in the confidence of and interest in the theorists of the Right. It is not that they have produced any new thinking, but simply that old ideas which seemed to have been crushed by the socialist juggernaut are now seen to be miraculously intact and ready to fill the intellectual vacuum which the newly-uncertain socialist thinkers have allowed to open up.

The Labour Party in Britain, traditionally and notoriously suspicious of ideas, is now paying the price for that lack of interest. It suddenly finds itself in a real battle of ideas and one that it is badly equipped to fight. It can no longer rely on the inevitability of victory. Fabian gradualism seems both too gradual and not very attractive when we get there. Socialism as a rather pleasant exercise in distributing the fruits of ever-increasing wealth according to high moral principles no longer seems available or practicable. The only ideology on offer is an out-dated and profoundly unattractive re-working of what Marx wrote a century ago or Trotsky said in 1938.

Yet the Labour Party is by tradition and force of circumstance a Party of the Left. It necessarily stands for some alternative view of how society should be organised. For the Labour Party, policy is not enough. It is not enough to pluck pragmatic solutions to practical problems out of the air. People are entitled to say that surely, for the Labour Party, policy is a means to an end, to an overall concept of society, and to enquire what that overall concept might be. The problem for the Labour Party at present is that we have little idea of what answer to give and, to the extent that we have an inkling of what the answer could be, we dare not give it, because we don't ourselves like it much and fear with good reason that neither would the electorate.

The problem is exacerbated by the fact that as Labour's broad-based support dwindles, and as its ideological armoury is denuded, the Party becomes more and more dependent for its dynamism on a small number of activists whose importance, both numerically and politically, grows proportionately to the decline of the Party as a whole. Activists are by definition unrepresentative. This would not matter too much in the case of a political party which takes an élitist view of political action, but it is totally inappropriate to a party whose *raison d'être* is its claim to represent, and act as the instrument of, the broad mass of ordinary people in society.

In the past, Labour Party activists have been aware of this problem and have striven to keep the links between them and Labour (non-activist) voters in good repair. But there are some elements in today's Labour Party who have no such concerns; they positively welcome and seek an élitist role, in which a frankly unrepresentative vanguard Party pushes out ahead of the mass of its supporters and, at the extreme, is actually engaged in a form of conspiracy against them. The view of society, and of the Party's role in it, which is being shaped by these people increases the divergence between the Party and its supporters and, by giving substance to the warnings of our opponents, is exactly the wrong and least appropriate response to the growing concern of potential Labour voters that in some ill-defined way the Labour Party is not to be trusted with the freedoms they wish to enjoy.

SOCIALISM AND FREEDOM

The problem of individual liberty in a socialist society has concerned socialist thinkers and writers ever since a corpus of socialist thought first emerged. It is even more pressing today than it has been in the past. In an advanced and sophisticated society, with high material living standards, what may seem in less advanced societies to be nice questions of abstract theory quite rightly assume an added importance. It is one of the ironies of the situation that many of those who have brought about this heightened awareness and who are vigilant to preserve the gains already made would claim to be socialists.

One of the problems is that such work as is currently being done on the subject is being undertaken inside academic institutions, far removed from the harsh realities of practical politics. It is published in journals with specialist readerships and in a jargon-ridden language which is not accessible to the ordinary reader. There is virtually no contact between the academic socialist theorist and the Labour Party politician. Yet the continued viability of the Labour Party, and of socialist principles, as instruments of governmental action, depend crucially on infusing practical programmes for political action with an understanding of the philosophical issues involved.

It may seem fanciful to suggest that the Labour Party canvasser on the doorstep will suffer, and has suffered, from the Party's failure to grapple successfully with apparently highly abstract questions of freedom and its compatibility with socialism. Yet he will be dimly aware of an intellectual vacuum at the heart of the Party's position; he will know that the intellectual ground has shifted under his feet; he will know that the old moral and intellectual certainties about the superiority of socialism as an ideal have been overtaken by an intellectual revolution in which a resurgent Right have captured the popular imagination and popular support.

There can be nothing more damaging to a Party which claims to offer a vision of a better society than to lose confidence in what that vision should be. No one doubts that socialism offers what is, in many respects, even to its opponents, a noble concept of how society should work. The question is whether, despite the nobility of the end which is sought, the means for achieving it inevitably require the suppression of individual liberty. Until we can give a clear, confident and reassuring answer to this question, we can expect socialism to become, in advanced Western societies, an historical relic rather than a hope for the future.

The notion that socialist advance can be achieved only at the expense of a loss of individual freedom is firmly entrenched, even amongst those who would willingly pay the price. Socialists have for long looked on with equanimity as their opponents have appropriated the slogans of freedom to themselves. It is now axiomatic that 'freedom of choice', 'free enterprise', and 'individual freedom' are all concepts – or at least labels – which are the property of the Right.

This has been accepted, partly as a result of empirical observation of the repressive nature of the self-proclaimed socialist regimes of Eastern Europe, China and the Third World, and partly because skilful propaganda use has been made of the Labour Party's lack of sensitivity to the issue in domestic politics, but, more importantly, because the tradition-al libertarian critique of socialist or collective action as necessarily incompatible with individual liberty has recently gained renewed currency.

That critique is firmly rooted in the free market economics of Adam Smith, the liberalism of John Stuart Mill and the *laissez-faire* purity of Herbert Spencer. In the post-war world, these ideas have been given new expression by writers like Friedman, Hayek and Nozick. It is not that the ideas themselves are new or are based on a new analysis; it is rather that they seem newly relevant to the conditions which have emerged, particularly over the past decade or so.

The supposed failure of Keynesian economics to deal with the oil-price shock to the Western economy meant that economic doctrines which had been discredited for decades and had lain dormant and ignored were suddenly called back to the centre of the stage. The revival of classical economics took the label of monetarism; but monetarism is not primarily an economic theory. It is rather an expression of political principle, and in its train has come a wholesale revival of interest in the political and philosophical beliefs of those who seized the opportunity to exploit the disarray and discomfort of the hitherto dominant progressive intellectuals.

This close relationship between political doctrines and economic prescriptions should come as no surprise. Socialists, particularly of the Marxist variety, have always argued that political power is inseparable from economic organisation; and their opponents have been equally quick to draw political lessons from the writings of Adam Smith. Modern writers like Friedman and Hayek make the connection even more explicit; and much of the recent attack on socialism is based on the view that central planning and state intervention in the economy, which are held to be integral to any socialist approach, are incompatible, not only with the economic freedom, but also with the civil and political liberties, of the individual.

It is generally argued that man as an individual is free, but that as soon as he enters society he necessarily sacrifices a part of that freedom in order to gain the benefits of social co-operation and organisation. The extent to which that freedom is given up is of course a matter of degree. It is usually thought that there is a trade-off between the benefit to the individual of retaining the maximum degree of personal freedom *vis-à-vis* the rest of society, and the benefit to society as a whole (and, in socialist theory, hence to the individual in society) of the greatest degree of rational co-operation.

Socialists have tended to accept that this trade-off exists, and have argued for the priority of the community as opposed to the individual interest on the ground that the benefits thereby obtained are more valuable than, and to some extent compensate for and replace, the lost advantages to the individual – advantages which are, in any case, very often illusory except to a privileged few. Socialists have preferred to draw attention to other types of freedom – freedom *from* hunger, poverty and ill-health – rather than the freedom of choice and freedom from coercion to which the Right attaches importance.

In this, the Left has conceded too much too easily and has not taken seriously enough the gravamen of the charge made by its opponents. This has begun to matter a great deal; as the old confidence about the positive virtues of socialism has diminished, the carelessness with which we have glossed over the alleged defects has counted against us more and more. People's perception of socialism in action has added to the Left's problems in this regard. In today's Britain, the Labour Party is too easily associated with entrenched interests, with the shoring up of out-dated power structures and with the placing of people in categories from which it is difficult to escape.

Too often, the Labour Party's policies – though well-intentioned – seem to be at variance with the ideals of socialism. It is the Labour Party which seems to say, in effect, to a large proportion of society 'You are council tenants and that's how you stay'; or 'You are trade union members and you damned well do what your leaders tell you.' The Labour Party's disregard of the theoretical problems of reconciling socialism with liberty is reflected in these policy difficulties, which alienate many of those whose interests Labour claim to represent and at the same time make it easier for our opponents to exploit a growing area of concern.

Socialism's opponents have in the main argued two distinct positions. In the first, there is also an acceptance of the trade-off; but the most desirable outcome is held to be the maintenance of the maximum degree of personal liberty, even at the expense of a less efficient, humane and equal social organisation. This view is justified on the basis of the overwhelming importance and value of liberty as compared with other social goods; the loss of material comfort and social justice are thought to be acceptable sacrifices for the sake of the higher ideal.

The second position is more comprehensive. The notion of the trade-off is rejected altogether; it is regarded as a snare and a delusion. According to this view, both individual liberty and wider social benefits are best guaranteed – indeed, can only be guaranteed – by concentrating exclusively on the overriding priority of freedom, not just because freedom is reckoned to be intrinsically superior as a social ideal to other objectives like justice and equality, but because the preservation of freedom is the only mechanism by which these other aims can be secured.

Socialists have traditionally been content to enter the lists against libertarians of the first school. They have been confident that the social advantages of community action would outweigh the assumed and marginal losses of individual liberty.

That comfortable and easily defended position is denied them when they are confronted with those who argue the second position. The argument becomes not one of choosing a point on a continuum – that is, essentially one of degree or of negotiation – so much liberty for so much social justice – but rather a clash between absolutes. The hearts and minds which are the prize in the argument must decide, not what balance they wish to strike between freedom and social justice, but whether both are furthered or destroyed by socialism.

Socialists are essentially on the defensive in this argument, mainly because they have failed to develop a position of attack. They are able to argue on equal terms when the question concerns how much liberty should be given up for how much social justice, but they can only defend when the charge is that socialism inevitably destroys freedom and, in consequence, makes impossible the achievement of other social goals. They have not so far developed a counter-attack which enables them to argue the converse of their opponents' position.

The counter-attack would require an argument to the effect that there is no trade-off between liberty on the one hand and social justice, equality, and efficiency on the other (to this extent accepting the fundamental premise of the opponents, and eschewing the treacherous concession implicit in the traditional socialist position), but that only by giving priority to the ideals of equality and justice is it possible to guarantee to everyone the maximum possible degree of individual liberty. This study is intended to provide the broad outlines of such an argument.

2 What Is Freedom?

INTRODUCTION

Robinson Crusoe was a free man. He was unable to escape from his island and he suffered all sorts of physical and material deprivations; but no boss or policeman or bureaucrat could tell him what to do and he owed no obligations to any one. He was, in the sense of the term which is crucial to our discussion, free.

When he was joined by Man Friday, his situation improved in various ways. But did his relationship with Man Friday and his acceptance that certain objectives could best be achieved by collective action mean that he suffered a diminution, admittedly a marginal one, of his freedom? He was no longer entirely the master of his own actions; the interests of someone other than himself also had to be considered. In return for the benefits of his relationship with Man Friday, he undertook obligations which arguably restricted his freedom to act as he alone thought fit. Did this mean, in any sense that matters, that he was less free?

If, of course, he had been taken prisoner or required to pay tribute or restricted to a certain part of the island by the natives who visited it from time to time, we should have little difficulty in agreeing that he had suffered a loss of freedom. But when he voluntarily circumscribed his movements on the island in order to avoid detection, was he less free? Was this limitation on his movements the equivalent of the physical confines imposed by geography? Did the fact that it was in a sense self-imposed, or at least was not deliberately imposed by someone else, mean that, while it reduced his practical scope, it did not limit his freedom?

NOT AN ABSOLUTE

The mere consideration of these questions immediately signals to us that the concept of freedom is a slippery and a complicated one. We must recognise that freedom is often a matter of degree and we have to decide what degree of restriction, and restrictions of what kind and for what purposes, should properly be regarded as impinging significantly on freedom.

Even in a society which is generally regarded as free, people who value their freedom accept a whole range of limitations – man-made limitations – which undeniably limit their freedom. The most obvious example is freedom of speech. In most countries which regard themselves as free, freedom of speech is substantially limited. In modern Britain, for example, there are the limitations imposed by rules regarding defamation, obscenity, sedition, racial hatred, blasphemy and so on. Yet most people in Britain would claim to enjoy freedom of speech.

This is not to say that the limitations on freedom of speech do not matter or are not real limitations. A racial bigot or an anti-monarchist, for example, would rightly regard his freedom of speech as being severely limited; and there can be no doubt that he is a less free person as a result – as are we all, since a freedom which we think we may not wish to exercise is nevertheless a freedom.

Let us look at a further example. Most people in Britain accept the obligation to drive on the left-hand side of the road, without regarding it as a restriction on their freedom. This general view is taken, not because the rule is not a limitation of freedom, but because its effect as a restriction is thought to be outweighed by its value as a social regulator. Most people acknowledge that, in the interest of safe and efficient traffic circulation, some such rule or restriction must apply.

What these examples show is that, even in a society which attaches value to the concept of individual liberty, some limitations on freedom are generally acceptable. The arguments arise about how extensive those limitations can be and about the justifications which can be advanced for them.

It is possible to identify a number of factors which lead people to regard restrictions as being acceptable, even when freedom is limited; indeed, their acceptability often obscures the fact that they have anything to do with freedom at all. Thus, the facts that (a) the restriction is generally willed or accepted (b) it is generally applicable, is fair and is not arbitrary or capricious in its application (c) it is seen as being for the public good and (d) it is seen as arising naturally and inevitably from man's role in society, will all help to reconcile people to accepting a limitation on their freedom.

The extent of this acceptability can often be, potentially if not actually, a matter of dispute, since it may be strongly conditioned by social and political factors which are themselves potentially controversial. The loss of freedom which an employee suffers in relation to his employer, for example, is not generally regarded as making the employee less free, because it is accepted as a necessary aspect of social and economic organisation. Yet the whole concept of the wage bargain could be challenged; and if that challenge were successful, in terms of showing the wage relationship to be neither inevitable nor desirable as a means of organising economic activity, it would also become much more vulnerable to attack on grounds of the restriction it necessarily imposes on individual liberty.

In deciding questions about freedom in society, we are therefore not only making judgments about the quantity of freedom which is desirable or acceptable but also about the relative values of different kinds of freedom and of different kinds of justification. The number and complexity of these variables should warn us against making glib pronouncements and easy judgments.

In order to meet the challenge of those who deny the compatibility of socialism and freedom, however, we are nevertheless obliged to try to establish some sort of basis on which the degree of freedom in society can be evaluated. Our first task is to identify those factors which are relevant to a proper definition of freedom.

A SOCIAL PHENOMENON

The human condition is sharply circumscribed by all sorts of limitations – those arising from the rules of time and space, from mortality, from natural endowments of intelligence, strength and so on. These naturally occurring limitations, which are intrinsic to the human condition, are not normally regarded as being relevant to freedom. Someone who is unable to arrive in Mars tomorrow, or to run a three minute mile, or to live for a thousand years, or to solve the mysteries of the universe, may regret these incapacities but he would not normally describe or consider himself to be less free as a result.

There might be circumstances where we might say that a man's freedom had been affected by some natural event, such as the blowing shut of a door so that he was accidentally locked in, but this somewhat strains the normal sense of the word and is in any case not the concept of freedom with which we are concerned. For our purposes – we are, after all, inquiring into the effect upon individual freedom of social arrangements – freedom, or rather the lack of it, is a social concept. It is relevant only to man in society.

In principle, a man outside society is totally free. Whatever the natural limitations which apply to him, including those which arise as a consequence of his own deficiencies, he is free – that is, no human or social agency limits the range of choice left to him by naturally occurring circumstances.

When he enters society, however, he accepts, as the price of the social benefits he gains, a number of social constraints upon his freedom of choice and action. This is because one of the principal objects and tasks of social organisation is, as the price of securing the benefits of social co-operation, to reconcile conflicting interests and to apportion relatively scarce resources; in order to achieve these objects, each individual must accept restrictions of his own freedom in return for similar concessions made by others in society. It is the nature and extent of those socially ordained restrictions which are the proper subject of our inquiry into the levels of freedom available in particular societies.

Constraints imposed upon one individual by another, unless that other acts with the sanction of the social organisation, will not generally count as limitations upon freedom, at least in any sense that is relevant to the assessment of the degree of freedom in a particular society. Thus, an isolated assault on or the imprisonment of one individual by another will not in any ordinary sense be said to have diminished the level of freedom in society, unless the assailant acts with the authority of society or in accordance with the rules (or absence of rules) prevailing in that society.

If freedom is to be defined in terms of constraints imposed on the individual by society, as opposed to those arising from natural limitations or imposed other than by socially ordained arrangements, what do we mean by 'society' and 'the individual' in this context?

Most writers assume that, for the purposes of defining the individual's freedom, it is the limitations imposed on a particular individual by the state and by other organised manifestations of the power of society as a whole which matter. There is equally a good measure of agreement that the individual loses freedom to the extent that he makes concessions, voluntarily or otherwise, to some collective body of which he is a member.

'Society' in this sense makes demands on the individual, and, to the extent that these demands are met, the individual's freedom is reduced. The relationship between the two parties is relatively simple and is not reciprocal. Society limits and the individual concedes freedom; the trade in freedom is all one way. It is always the individual's, not society's, freedom which is at stake and which is conceded. It is the loss of individual freedom in this sense – as a consequence of demands made of the individual by the state or by collective organisations – which is emphasised by right-wing writers.

But what of constraints imposed on the individual by other individuals under rules formulated and enforced – or in accordance with practices (such as racist or sexist discrimination) permitted – by society? Are not other individuals in the same position for the purposes of this analysis as other elements in society? Is not one individual entitled to argue, in the name of his claim to freedom, that that freedom must be preserved as much against other individuals as against social organisations of various sorts?

The reason that many people do not readily answer this question in the affirmative, as is surely correct, is that, in the case of the relationship between one individual and another in society, the trade in freedom is, potentially at least, two-way. The individual may at the same time defend his own freedom and be a claimant on the freedom of others. Each individual in society, in other words, has a simple relationship with 'society' but a more complex, two-way relationship with each other individual in society.

This point is constantly overlooked and consequently misunderstood by right-wing writers. They treat the relationship between one individual and others as equivalent to, and as simple as, that between the individual and 'society' (the state or the collective), at least in the sense that it can be looked at solely from the viewpoint of the one individual whose freedom is under consideration – that is, from only one end of a two-way relationship.

This is surely to ignore the complex balancing which must occur in a free society between one individual's rights and those of all other individuals. An immunity from the constraints imposed by other individuals can easily mean a diminution in the freedom enjoyed by those others; and while this may seem an admirable extension of individual liberty when looked at from the viewpoint of the individual claiming the immunity, it may seem a retrograde step when the same relationship is looked at from the viewpoint of the other individuals who are party to it.

Nozick is typical in this respect of those so-called libertarians who insist on discussing freedom from the viewpoint of one given individual in relation to society as a whole, without appearing to recognise that the freedom of each individual will turn on his relations, not just with 'society' but with each other individual in society.

He takes as his starting point the extent of the freedom enjoyed by 'the' individual before he enters society and then examines the purposes for which that individual would agree to give up some elements of that ideal freedom in return for the benefits of social co-operation. He is particularly concerned with the position of that individual who prizes his freedom above all else and will cede it only for the most pressing reason, and he concludes that the claims which society can legitimately make on such an individual's freedom are extremely limited.

Nozick argues for the 'night watchman' state which provides only the most minimal services to society and makes the smallest possible demands on the individual's freedom of action and choice. He says that any attempt to go further than this and to aim at a social end result, in conformity with equality or any other social principle, would require a degree of interference in freedom to which the individual would not rationally agree.

For Nozick, therefore, any attempt to secure social justice or to establish equality or to achieve any other pre-determined social pattern must necessarily reduce individual liberty. The only responsibility that can properly be undertaken by society in this regard is to see that, whatever the eventual or changing distribution of powers, rights and obligations may be, it is carried through according to socially determined rules of procedural justice, so that, for example, people are not arbitrarily deprived of their property.

But provided that people part with their property voluntarily, in return for other benefits and in accordance with just rules, no one can complain if some people accumulate, as a result of greater talent and other capacities, more property and power than others. The natural distribution of power will inevitably be unequal and unpredictable; it can be made to conform to a pattern only by interfering with the freedom of those who would naturally and justly have broken its bounds.

This is certainly an arguable position if we insist on looking at the question of freedom from the viewpoint of just one individual, especially if that individual happens to be one who would naturally accumulate power and privilege. He might well argue, in line with Nozick, that any attempt to reduce his rights and powers in accordance with some pre-determined social objective would limit his freedom.

As we shall see, however, this is far too narrow a view of how freedom is to be measured; freedom in society is something which matters to each individual. We do not satisfactorily answer the question as to how free is society by looking at the situation of just one of its members; the answer to that question must depend on the situation of every member and that will be affected by the claims made by each other member.

POSITIVE FREEDOM

If we are agreed that freedom in society is to be defined and measured according to the constraints imposed on any given individual by all other human and social agencies in society, including other individuals acting in accordance with the rules established by that society, there remain major questions about the form that those constraints might take. We shall look at those questions later, but we must first try to identify what it is that is left encompassed once all the constraints upon freedom have been taken into account.

There are those (among them, Berlin, whose views we shall consider shortly) who prefer to define freedom negatively, so that it means simply the absence of constraint. This is perfectly accurate so far as it goes, but the attempt to characterise the positive aspects of freedom may nevertheless help us to a better understanding of what freedom means.

The major problem in defining freedom positively is to distinguish the concept of freedom from the consequences of exercising freedom. As we shall see later, freedom has no meaning unless it is capable of being exercised; it is therefore easy to understand the view that the manifestation of freedom, and the evidence for its existence, lie in the consequences of its exercise.

But there are difficulties in taking this approach. The notion of exercising a freedom inevitably implies the doing of something positive. It is but a short step then to equate freedom with the notion of a positive action – and very often, positive in this context may itself have a dual meaning, denoting both an action or decision to do something, as opposed to inaction or a decision to do nothing, and a doing of something that is positive in the sense of being constructive in a teleological sense.

In fact, freedom is quite separate from the consequences of its exercise, and it should certainly not be equated with the positive doing of something. Let us assume that I am capable of lifting a heavy weight, or of becoming a great painter. In both cases, what we describe in that statement is my power or capacity to do those things. If I choose to do them, I exercise that power or capacity; but my freedom to do them does not consist in my doing them but in my ability to choose to do them, or not, or only partially, as the case may be. The question of my freedom to do them does not arise, in other words, unless my ability to choose whether or not to exercise my power or capacity is threatened by some socially ordained constraint.

Let us make the same point in a different way. If we imagine that the various constraints which are relevant to freedom in a negative sense define and circumscribe a physical area, then our freedom consists in our ability to move to any point within that area. Our freedom lies, however, not in the positive act of going to some point, and even less in going to a particular point, but in our ability to choose whether to go to any point or indeed to stay where we are.

The failure to distinguish between the exercise of a power or capacity (which consists in actually doing something) and the exercise of a freedom (which consists in choosing whether or not to exercise a power or capacity) has bedevilled the whole concept of freedom in its positive sense. It is this failure, and the consequent tendency to regard freedom as a positive power, with connotations of self-improvement and the perfectability of man, which is strongly attacked by Berlin.

He argues that this view of positive freedom too easily becomes distorted and develops into a doctrine which produces the very antithesis of freedom. He does not say that there is any logically inevitable connection between positive freedom and the doctrines which he attacks, but he does say that there is a natural tendency for the one to develop into the other.

This natural tendency arises because those who argue that freedom is about the development of the human potential will often attach to this view two further concepts – that there is within each person an ideal and perfectly rational inner self with whom in ordinary circumstances the individual will be in conflict but who can, in a state of freedom, be released and allowed to develop, and secondly, that the cosmos enjoys a perfect harmony and unity so that all virtues and values must be compatible with each other and form a harmonious whole.

It is true that it is but a short step from views of this sort to the notion that man can be led to freedom, even against his will, by being shown ways in which he can fully realise his inner potential, resolve any conflict within himself and establish his place in a harmonious cosmos; in such a society, man would be 'forced to be free'.

Berlin is right to say that this dangerous error is much facilitated by those who fail to distinguish between freedom defined positively (the ability to choose) and the concept of doing something positive. Interestingly, however, the concept of negative freedom also makes a contribution to this distortion of what freedom really means.

Freedom negatively defined, as Berlin would prefer, implies a potential conflict between what the individual chooses and the constraints which may be imposed upon him. That conflict arises most naturally where the individual chooses to do something which he is prevented from doing, rather than when he chooses not to do something; it is therefore easy to slip into the error, even where the starting point is the concept of negative freedom, of assuming that freedom is a matter of realising one's personal potential – that is, of doing something positive – which might be frustrated by the imposition of constraints.

The conflict between choice and constraint is equally real and equally destructive of freedom, however, if the individual is prevented from exercising his choice to do nothing. Freedom must of course include the power to choose to be lazy, to make less of oneself than one might, to be irrational, to opt out, to be evil and so on, as well as the power to develop fully one's personal capacities.

NEGATIVE FREEDOM

There is, however, a more fundamental objection to Berlin's treatment of liberty. Because he is suspicious of positive liberty, he prefers to define freedom in a negative sense, in terms of the absence of constraint. He rightly excludes from those constraints which define negative liberty those which arise naturally or outside society; but, in asserting that the only constraints which are relevant are those produced by deliberate human coercion, he thereby purports to exclude all those social and economic inequalities which are the more or less indirect consequences of our political and social arrangements.

In this, he is strongly endorsed by those, like Hayek and Nozick, who wish to argue that direct interventions by the state are the principal limitations of freedom, and that shifts in the balance of advantage between individuals in society are rarely relevant to freedom. If this view prevails, the way is clear to treating equality and freedom as, at best, divergent and, at worst, incompatible.

The socialist, on the other hand, would wish to argue that where people suffer comparative deprivations of various sorts, particularly in the economic field, and those deprivations are the inevitable consequence of socially ordained arrangements, these are factors which can be regarded as limiting the freedom of the individuals affected.

As we have seen, freedom is a social concept, and Berlin is right to say that only those constraints which are socially created are relevant. The disputed area concerns those constraints, largely economic in nature, which are neither natural (since they are clearly social in origin) nor directly coercive (since they arise, arguably at any rate, only as the result of the interplay of many factors among which social arrangements are perhaps not the most important), but which undeniably have an important bearing on the individual's capacity to exercise choice.

If the socialist can make good his claim that this category of constraints is relevant to the definition of freedom, the consequences will be far-reaching. The widest possible distribution and highest possible level of individual freedom would thereby become not only consistent with, but achievable only by, a socialist drive for equality across a wide range of social and economic activity. The Rawlsian dividing line between freedom (to be distributed equally) and other social and economic benefits (to be subjected to the difference principle) would have to be drawn at a somewhat different point from that which Rawls had in mind. These questions are much more fully developed in a later chapter.

In the introduction to his *Four Essays on Freedom*, Berlin concedes that freedom of choice and action are affected for many people by economic considerations; but these considerations are, he argues, not constraints upon freedom because they are not created by deliberate human coercion. They are relevant only as 'conditions of freedom' – defining the circumstances in which freedom may be exercised – rather than defining the limits of freedom itself.

If this is so, they seem very similar to the natural limitations upon human powers – the natural rules of time and space, mortality, variations in natural endowments, and so on – which everyone concedes do not arise from man's position in society and therefore have nothing to do with freedom. Yet, significantly, Berlin does not attempt, as he might, to make this analogy. He implicitly concedes, therefore, that such constraints are social rather than natural in origin and, in consequence, potentially coercive.

How convincing is Berlin's attempted distinction between coercive constraints upon freedom and socially ordained, non-natural conditions affecting the exercise of freedom? Or, to put it another way, is the deliberate human coercion identified by Berlin an essential element of the constraints which define freedom?

We should immediately concede that 'conditions of freedom'

are not necessarily just constraints upon freedom. An inability to feed oneself, for example, has a significance which transcends any consideration of freedom alone. They establish the context in which not only freedom but many other – perhaps fundamental – aspects of the human condition do or do not exist. But the fact that they can be more than a constraint upon freedom does not mean that they are not relevant to the definition of freedom as well.

The absence or denial of a 'condition of freedom', if it prevents the exercise of that freedom and is socially ordained, must surely be a constraint upon freedom. This is because freedom is not, at bottom, an abstract, but rather a practical, thing. A freedom without the practical possibility of its being exercised is no freedom at all and has no meaning. It would be as paradoxical as a sight that could not be seen.

Berlin appears to duck this point in his unwillingness to give anything like a positive meaning to the concept of freedom. Yet, even if we insist on defining freedom solely in negative terms, we must still concede that what is left enclosed within the constraints which limit freedom is surely the ability to exercise choice in thought and action – a choice which to be real and to exist at all must be capable of being exercised.

If a socially created factor, such as poverty or hunger or unemployment, limits the power to choose, it cannot be regarded as at the same time relevant to freedom (because socially created) and yet not a constraint upon freedom. If it is, in Berlin's terminology, a condition of freedom, in the sense that it limits the *exercise* of freedom, then it is a constraint upon freedom, since freedom in its positive sense can have no meaning except as something which can be exercised.

Rather than accept Berlin's implied contention that there is a three-fold classification – natural constraints, conditions of freedom and deliberate coercions – it seems more logical therefore to postulate a two-fold classification – those constraints which are natural and unavoidable, and are therefore not relevant to the concept of freedom, (though even here it could be argued that, to the extent that natural handicaps could be mitigated by social action, society's failure to do so might be regarded as deliberate) and those which, being man-made and socially ordained, are properly to be regarded as constraints upon freedom. Deliberate coercion would be simply one example of this latter category.

Berlin recognises the force of this point by conceding that some do regard these economic constraints or 'conditions of freedom' as relevant to freedom. He himself is unable to endorse this view because, he says, it depends on a partisan analysis (which he does not agree with) of the ways in which different economic and social systems operate. In other words, he implies that such an argument is an expression of a particular political viewpoint rather than of any universal truth about political or social systems in general.

Berlin does not appear to deny that some economic constraints could in some circumstances limit freedom. What he appears to be saying is that socially created economic constraints in general need not be regarded as coercive, that for this reason they are not relevant to freedom, and that the sounder view is that this is the case in our own society.

But this seems to be a difficult position to sustain. Either the imposition of economic constraints is an inevitable feature and consequence of all social organisations, in which case the proposition that they are imposed by society is no longer one depending on a partisan analysis of particular societies but is universally true. Or, they are not an inevitable feature of all social arrangements, in which case a society such as our own which clearly does impose such constraints (as Berlin concedes, when he identifies them as 'conditions of freedom' in contra-distinction to natural limitations) must be regarded as choosing to impose them and thereby, in Berlin's terminology, coercing those on whom they are imposed.

The only escape open to Berlin is to adopt the inherently implausible position that some societies do impose economic constraints but that ours does not. He does not, however, attempt to argue this, presumably because even the most ardent proponent of a market-based, capitalist or mixed economy would surely concede that one of its chief characteristics and mechanisms is the creation of economic inequalities, through the provision of incentives to some and the correlative imposition of constraints upon others – by encouraging some, for example, to accumulate capital which can be used to employ others who, by definition, do not have capital and cannot be employers.

Nor does he attempt to argue that the market is a natural phenomenon which occurs independently of society and therefore is not a social arrangement. He presumably recognises that the market is not something which arises naturally, but is a means of allocating scarce resources and reconciling conflicts of interest – exactly the objects of every form of social organisation. It depends for its workings on a whole series of man-made rules and institutions – the concept of private property, the right of inheritance, the law of contract, the limited liability company, and so on.

The many forms of non-market societies which have existed and still exist show that we could, if we wish, choose to resolve these problems differently. The fact that the scale and distribution of economic constraints is differently organised from one society to another shows that these factors are socially created and are therefore amenable to change and limitation by social action. To remove them or to reduce them substantially may be difficult and require the sacrifice of other social objectives, such as efficiency, but there can be no doubt that economic constraints, in the sense of economic disadvantages which apply to some but not to others, could be much reduced. The extent to which they are not so reduced must be regarded as the deliberate consequence of social arrangements.

If it does not seem possible to argue that economic constraints are not socially ordained, can it then be said that, because any society is bound to produce economic constraints, those which we find in our own society can properly be omitted from a consideration of freedom? The universality and inevitability of economic constraints in society surely does not entitle us to ignore them. Rather, the nature and degree of these constraints must be entered into the balance sheet when the degree of freedom enjoyed in that society is calculated. Berlin might wish to argue (though he does not) that the economic constraints imposed on some of its members by our society are less onerous than in other societies, but that is rather different from arguing (as he does) that they do not exist or do not matter.

If economic constraints are created by all societies, and undeniably in our own, how is it possible for Berlin and others to regard them as non-coercive, in the sense of not being the inevitable consequence of social organisation? The answer lies in the complex nature of economic powers and in the sophisticated methods our modern society has devised for allocating them. As a consequence, economic constraints are much more difficult to recognise, by comparison with the more straightforward constraints upon physical liberty and political rights.

There can in fact be no doubt that economic constraints can be just as coercive as other forms of constraint. The point can be made clearly if we imagine a social order which denies to certain classes of people the power to act as economic agents. If, for example, it were decreed that no blue-eyed person was allowed to work, or to enter into commercial transactions, or to earn more than a certain amount, we should have little difficulty in characterising that as a coercive constraint upon liberty. The point is not hypothetical; in our own society, coercive economic powers are actually exercised by employers, landlords, monopoly suppliers and so on. But there are many factors which serve to obscure this simple point.

First, the capacity to act as an economic agent is seen to be intrinsic to the human condition; to the extent that it undeniably depends on personal attributes and natural endowments, it is perceived to arise independently of and to be largely unaffected by social arrangements or rules.

This means that the effect of social arrangements on economic powers is difficult to recognise and measure because those powers will naturally vary from one individual to another; the further variations caused or reinforced by socially imposed constraints are hard to disentangle from the differences which exist naturally. Unlike physical freedom or political rights, which are easily recognised because they either exist or do not, economic freedoms have much less clear contours.

Conversely, it could be argued that it is precisely the socially created nature of economic benefits which means that conferring those benefits unequally – so that some get less than others – cannot be regarded as a constraint upon those who get less, since they are still net beneficiaries. But if we draw a parallel with political and civil rights, which are also the product of social organisation, we can see that the deprivation or unequal distribution of those rights is clearly to be regarded as a loss of freedom. The withdrawal or diminution of a socially created benefit, whether in the political or economic field, must be regarded as a socially created constraint.

The fact that economic powers depend partly on natural attributes and partly on social arrangements should not pose any logical obstacle to regarding limitations of them as constraints upon freedom. We have no difficulty in recognising a restriction on the purely natural ability to move from one place to another as a constraint upon freedom. Nor do we have any problem with the removal of a political right, such as the right to vote, although this is entirely a socially created right. If constraints can be recognised at either end of a scale which leads from purely natural rights at one end to rights which are entirely created by social organisation at the other, there should be no difficulty in regarding as relevant those constraints which operate on powers which are partly natural and partly created by social arrangement.

A further obstacle to clear analysis is that many economic freedoms will have only the most marginal importance. I may not care very much whether, in addition to all the other things I choose to do with my purchasing power, I can also dine at the Ritz; I might therefore not easily recognise that particular deprivation as having much to do with my freedom. This does not mean that my lack of the additional economic power to dine at the Ritz is not potentially a constraint on my freedom, or that for some people and in some circumstances it might not be a freedom which they value. In other words, the marginality – even the hypothetical nature – of many economic freedoms (the list is, after all, virtually limitless) does not disqualify all economic constraints from being regarded as potential constraints upon freedom.

This leads us to a further point. What is or is not regarded as a constraint on freedom is often a matter of expectation. Expectations in this field are in turn largely the product of social conditions and of social conditioning. For example, a prohibition on the publication of political treatises would be more seriously regarded, and would be a more significant constraint on freedom, in a modern Western democracy than it would in a primitive society of illiterates.

Expectations in the political field are generally more clearly defined, in respect of freedoms such as the right to vote, or to belong to political organisations, than in the economic field where economic conditions are so variable. What constitutes economic freedom in a particular society is therefore much more difficult to identify and will vary very much more from one society to another.

Expectations will be strongly influenced by what is seen as being available to other members of that same society. If it is the norm for most people to have the economic power to obtain adequate health care for themselves, for example, others in that society may well develop expectations in that direction, and feel themselves deprived and therefore constrained if their expectations are disappointed. In other words, there will be a strong tendency in any society to measure economic freedom on a relative basis – relative, that is, to others in that society. This means that some concept of approximate equality will be an important factor in assessing freedom in the economic sphere.

Moreover, an economic constraint is rarely absolute. It usually takes the form of a reduced range of choice, rather than an absolute prohibition. A poor man might be able to buy a Rolls Royce, by sacrificing all other economic objectives, but it could not be argued on that basis that he had the same freedom to buy a Rolls Royce as a millionaire enjoys.

If this is right, however, and economic freedom is often simply a matter of the available range of economic choice, this appears to suggest that a rise in the price of a desired economic good might, by reducing the number of choices open to the individual, limit his freedom. It seems difficult at first sight to argue that a shopkeeper who, perhaps for very good reason, raises the price of bread is thereby limiting the freedom of his customers in any real sense.

The point is less difficult than it appears. First, in a market economy, a rise in price which reflects factors such as greater scarcity (for example, following a crop failure) or a change in relative production costs might be treated as a more or less natural phenomenon and falling outside the range of constraints which are socially created and therefore relevant to freedom. Where, however, a price is increased by deliberate decision, either to achieve a planning objective in a planned economy or to exploit a market opportunity, the argument is a little different.

The proposition that the rise in price limits freedom in these circumstances seems doubtful only because the effect of raising a price will usually be so marginal as to have little effect on reducing choice. But Hayek and Nozick both concede that someone who unfairly exploits a monopoly of some essential commodity, such as bread or water, by demanding an outrageous price, can be regarded as limiting the freedom of those whose area of choice is reduced. Similarly, the reduction of choice for consumers through price increases may be treated as relevant to freedom when, in a centrally controlled economy, for example, the price of bread or meat is doubled overnight. In this case, the individual shopkeeper will be merely the agent for the economic system as a whole.

Perhaps the most important reason for failing to recognise economic deprivation as a constraint upon liberty is that such constraints are usually applied, in a modern society, indirectly rather than directly. If, for example, we are told that we cannot holiday in the West Indies because the authorities have withdrawn our passports, we should certainly feel that our freedom had been restricted. If, however, we should like to holiday in the West Indies but cannot afford it, we may regret our lack of purchasing power but we do not naturally think of ourselves as being any less free. It will seem part of the natural order of things.

Does it really make a difference, though, that those who suffer economic deprivation are not selected directly by some authority but are identified by impersonal processes? Let us imagine a society which is organised on the basis that one quarter of the population should act as slaves to the majority. Surely, the slaves would not be regarded as any the less un-free if it could be shown that they were selected periodically by competitive examination, or by some physical or other test, or by lottery. Nor would it make any difference to their freedom or lack of it to show that they could have avoided their enslaved condition if only they had been more skilled or deserving; nor would it matter that they might have a chance in the future of exchanging their position with someone who is currently free.

We should certainly have no hesitation in saying, in respect of such a society, that those who were for the time being enslaved were not free and that their lack of freedom meant that the society as a whole was less free than it otherwise might be. What matters here, surely, is not the precise identity of those who are enslaved, or even the processes by which they are selected, but the fact that the society is organised to produce that result.

Our judgment would not change, however much care was taken to make the process of selection fair, non-arbitrary, subject to procedural safeguards, and so on. Nor would it matter whether the social rules which produced this result were imposed by a dictator or were decided democratically or were simply accepted as natural by society as a whole.

Would it make any difference if those in positions of authority protested that it was not their direct intention that one quarter of the population should be enslaved – indeed, that they very much regretted it – but that society had to be organised in that way because otherwise some of the more onerous and less pleasant tasks in society would not get done, and then everyone would suffer? We should surely say that none of these pleas of mitigation would alter the simple fact that the prevailing social arrangement meant that some people suffered a significant loss of freedom.

What conclusions can we now reach? It seems clear that economic deprivation can be an important constraint on freedom, that this remains true despite the difficulty in many cases of recognising economic constraints as such, and that the organisation of society so that the constraints are imposed indirectly and impersonally does not render them any the less socially ordained. We must surely accept that, while there is certainly room for argument about what forms of economic deprivation might constitute constraints on freedom and while views on that may differ from one social situation to another, economic deprivation can, in some circumstances, be a constraint on freedom.

So far as economic deprivation for some people is the consequence of market arrangements, it must be regarded as a constraint which is imposed by a human or social agency. The market cannot be absolved from responsibility on the ground that it imposes such constraints in a fair, non-arbitrary, impersonal, generally acceptable way or that the imposition of those constraints is not the primary or even direct purpose of the market organisation of society.

Berlin is therefore wrong to dismiss market-created economic and social deprivation as being irrelevant to his concept of negative freedom. The seriousness and extent of constraints of this type, and the value of the freedoms thus limited, are clearly matters for debate; but there can surely be no doubt that a concept of freedom which overlooks these constraints is seriously defective.

What this means is that, in order to determine the degree of freedom in any particular society, we must look at substantial inequalities in social and economic powers, as well as the familiar constraints upon physical movement and political and civil rights. The denial to an individual of educational opportunity, or adequate health care, or decent housing or a reasonable income – measured comparatively against what is available to other people in that society – would have to be regarded as a constraint upon that individual's freedom – that is, upon his power to choose whether or not to exercise in society the powers and capacities which he possesses.

A society such as our own which appears to perform well on the more usual tests may be reckoned less free than we normally suppose when these additional tests are applied. And the traditional socialist concern with these matters would then have to be seen as an attempt to extend rather than to limit freedom.

MEASURING FREEDOM

We are now clear that freedom is, in its positive sense, the individual's ability to choose whether or not to exercise his powers and capacities, and that it is circumscribed and therefore defined by socially ordained constraints, including those which unequally deny to the individual social and economic powers which society makes available to others. Our next task is to ask whether freedom can be quantified and whether the quantity of freedom matters. In other words, does a given society satisfy the test to which we wish to subject it by providing only a certain minimum element of freedom or can we rank societies according to the amount of freedom which they permit to the individual?

We can quickly agree that it is possible to quantify freedom for the individual. If we imagine the freedom available to a given individual as being an area defined by the constraints imposed upon him by society, so that as constraints are imposed, the area becomes smaller, we can see that it is possible in principle to measure that area as it shrinks or grows, and therefore to quantify the amount of freedom available to that individual.

Should we distinguish between and award different values to

different kinds of freedom? Should we, for example, give a greater value to the more fundamental freedoms – such as freedom from political oppression or from hunger – than to the less commonly expected and available freedoms, such as the freedom to holiday in the West Indies? In other words, as freedom is diminished, so that the area of freedom becomes smaller, does what remains become more valuable? And does this mean that, if we start with two individuals enjoying equal freedoms, and then add to the freedom of one at the expense of another, what is added is less valuable than what is taken away?

There is surely a strong argument for asserting that there is indeed a hierarchy of freedoms, and that some freedoms are more fundamental and are worth more than others. Freedom is not, in practice, an infinitely expandable concept; once a reasonable degree of freedom is established, most people will be able to do most of what they reasonably expect to be able to do, and any further relaxation of the constraints upon their freedom will mean less to them than a tightening of the constraints would mean to a person with a lesser degree of freedom.

The heartland of freedom is, in other words, its most valuable territory. As the constraints on freedom are pushed back, so that it is possible to wander further afield, those outlying areas, while still important, have less value than the heartland. To deprive someone of all or a substantial part of his remaining small area of freedom for the sake of bestowing it upon someone who already enjoys a wider area of freedom can never be a satisfactory exchange. In measuring freedom, therefore, it is not simply the quantity that matters; attention must also be paid to the value of some freedoms as compared with others.

If freedom can be measured, does the measurement matter? The answer must again be a clear 'yes'. If the concept has any meaning or value, it must be better to have more rather than less, all other things being equal. There are of course possible trade-offs between freedom and other social objectives and these are frequently made. But our particular concern is with freedom, and it is the test of the extent of freedom which we wish to apply to socialist society; we are therefore entitled to ask whether socialism permits more or less freedom than is possible in other types of society, and to assert that a society which permits more rather than less freedom scores higher marks on our test.

But we have not yet solved the problem of how freedom is to be measured. We can measure the amount of freedom available to a given individual in society, but how is freedom in society as a whole to be measured? Do we simply aggregate the amount of freedom available to each individual? Or is the calculation more complicated?

It is certainly arguable that the aggregated total of individual freedoms should not be the only criterion. What are we to make, for example, of a society which scores well in terms of an overall total, but whose total is made up of a great deal of freedom for some but nil or very restricted freedom for others? Could we properly regard a society such as South Africa, or a society like Ancient Greece which permitted slavery, as free, even if the sum total of freedom was high? Should a society which claims to be free not guarantee to everyone at least an acceptable minimum of freedom to each individual?

These questions are valuable because they encourage us to think of freedom in terms of the individual rather than of society. It is in some senses a mistake to talk in terms of a society being free; it is the individual in society who is, or is not, free. Freedom matters and makes sense only in relation to the individual. A society can be said to be free only in the sense that the individuals who go to make up that society are free within that society.

It is difficult therefore to measure how free a society is, as an entity, in any meaningful sense. We can ask only how free is each individual in that society. And because the question is relevant to every individual, it has to be asked of every individual in that society. We cannot proclaim that a society is free if some individuals within it have less freedom than the generally accepted or expected norm. In those circumstances, we should have to say that while some individuals are free, others are not, or are less free; and that that lack of freedom means that society is less free than it would otherwise be.

It would matter little to this judgment whether or not it could be shown that the society had a high sum total of freedom or a high average degree of freedom. We should still be bound to say that, in the only sense in which freedom has any meaning – as a power exercised by the individual against society – some individuals in that society are not free. It is, in other words, the freedom of the least free (other than the obvious cases, such as the criminally insane) which is the central factor in the judgment we make of the extent of freedom in society as a whole.

The most free society will therefore be that in which the highest minimum degree of freedom is enjoyed. If we assume for the moment that there is a finite quantity of freedom to be distributed in society, then, in mathematical terms, the highest possible minimum is achieved by the highest possible average – and the highest possible average is achieved by an equal distribution.

This simple proposition can be tested (for the non-mathematical) by considering the disposition of 100 units among 10 people; the highest possible minimum share and the highest possible average share will both be achieved by an equal distribution of 10 to each person. The most free society will therefore be one in which freedom is equally distributed.

This proposition accords well with Rawls' concept of the sort of agreement people would reach in the 'original position' – where no one had any information about the natural advantages that each possessed. We shall look at Rawls' argument in more detail in a later chapter; we need note here only that Rawls argues that in the 'original position' people would insist that each person should have the maximum degree of freedom compatible with an equal degree of freedom for everyone else. His argument on this point is certainly persuasive, since it is difficult to believe that rational people with the power freely to reach agreement with each other would accept any other arrangement.

If we permitted a less equal distribution of freedom, so that some people had more than the highest possible average amount of freedom, then by definition others would enjoy less than that maximum average; the gain in freedom to some would be at least matched, in terms of quantity, and probably exceeded in terms of value, by a loss of freedom for others. This is undeniably true as a mathematical proposition; but it is also true because a degree of freedom which is greater than the average will always threaten to move into the area of what Hirsch calls positional goods. The exercise of freedom then becomes more in the nature of a privilege which can only be exercised at the expense of other people whose range of choice must be correspondingly limited. It is, in other words, a prejudicial privilege; the freedom, for example, to enjoy more than the usual degree of privacy or the beauty of an uninterrupted view can be secured only by excluding others.

Is equality of freedom all that maters? Are we entitled to assume that the total amount of freedom available in society is finite and invariable, so that the problem is simply one of distribution to the maximum advantage of a known quantity? Or is the amount of freedom in society variable or even limitless, in which case society would have to take two sorts of decisions – first, as to the best pattern of distribution, and secondly, as to the total quantity of freedom in relation perhaps to other social values?

In order to answer these questions, we must first decide whether there is any theoretical limit to the amount of freedom which the individual can enjoy. We can imagine a scale of freedom on which, as social constraints become more numerous and pervasive, the amount of freedom available to the individual declines; it could fall to the point where it is virtually extinguished. There is, however, an identifiable point at the top of the scale, when the last constraint is removed and the individual ceases to be subject to any demands made by other members or institutions of society. (This could be true only of someone who lived out of society or who was so powerful as to bend the whole of society to his will).

At that point, we have reached the theoretical maximum degree of freedom; nothing further can be done to add to the individual's freedom. We can therefore confidently assert that in measuring and distributing freedom we are dealing with a quantifiable and limited total.

That maximum degree of freedom which the individual may theoretically enjoy, however, bears little relationship to the maximum degree of freedom available in practice to individuals in society. The maximum possible total of freedom for society as a whole will be considerably less than the aggregate of the theoretical maxima for each individual. This is because it would be quite impossible for each individual in society to exercise the maximum degree of freedom theoretically available to a given individual, since diminutions of freedom will inevitably be required of and accepted by each individual in society – even in a society which claims to be relatively free – in relation to each other individual.

These considerations mean that there is an effective, as

opposed to a theoretical, maximum degree of freedom, even in a society which gives absolute priority to the maximisation of individual freedom. That effective maximum could be further reduced, however, if a given society chose to give greater priority to social objectives other than individual freedom. Those other social objectives might be, for example, military preparedness, productive efficiency, and so on.

The distribution of freedom is, in other words, not the only question society has to resolve in determining the amount of freedom available to the individual. Even where the total amount of freedom is distributed equally, so maximising the freedom available to each individual, society may have chosen to give a low priority to freedom and thereby have reduced the total amount of freedom available for distribution.

The critics of socialism maintain that this is precisely what a socialist society does. It is important, however, to analyse carefully the exact nature of this charge.

If it could be shown that a socialist society necessarily or habitually subordinates the maximisation of freedom to other social objectives, such as efficiency or the dominance of a particular group or class, then the charge would stick. Even then, it might be difficult to say that this was a characteristic peculiar to socialist societies, since there are undoubtedly many non-socialist examples of precisely this phenomenon.

This is not, however, the case which is usually made against socialism. The gravamen of that charge is usually that, in pursuing objectives which are specifically socialist, such as a high degree of social and economic equality, freedom is necessarily diminished, because individual freedom and equality in these respects are necessarily incompatible.

Yet we have already seen that the objective of achieving the greatest possible degree of equality in the distribution of freedom (including those social and economic benefits which are relevant to freedom) cannot possibly fall within the category of social objectives which may be traded-off against individual freedom. This is because, as we saw above, the greatest possible equality in the distribution of freedom is the means of maximising individual freedom in a given society; seeking equality of freedom cannot therefore run counter to giving overriding priority to freedom as a social objective.

The confusion in the anti-socialist case on this point possibly arises because the equalisation of freedom will provide otherwise disadvantaged individuals in society with a number of benefits, such as political power and the power to be active economically, as well as the maximum degree of freedom. These additional benefits have an independent value, and are relevant to freedom only when they are threatened by constraints imposed by social agencies, including other individuals.

Because, however, freedom is maximised by restricting the power of some individuals to limit the social and economic powers of others, it is easy to make the error of regarding the equalisation of freedom as being a trade-off exercise, in which the freedom of some individuals is reduced in return, let us say, for greater economic security for others. The anti-socialist critic then proclaims, on the basis of this error, that a socialist society is one in which freedom is subordinated to another social goal – that is, to social and economic equality.

In truth, however, the equalisation of freedom is to be justified, as we have seen, in terms of *maximising* freedom; the trade-off is between freedom and freedom (the more extensive and therefore less valuable freedoms of some being limited in order to provide fundamental freedoms to everyone). The further (and to some extent incidental) social benefits of equalising freedom, such as economic security or political rights for all, are merely alternative ways of expressing the concept of the maximum effective degree of individual freedom.

In principle, therefore, there is nothing in the socialist goal of greater equality which threatens freedom in society; indeed, the opposite is true, since only by equalising freedom and the political, social and economic powers which are relevant to it can the highest possible degree of individual freedom be obtained.

In practice, however, there are pitfalls of which the socialist must beware. Just as in a capitalist or liberal market society, there is wide agreement on the importance of equalising those political powers which are relevant to freedom, but an almost complete blind spot in respect of equally relevant social and economic powers, so, in many socialist societies, the reverse is true; there is great emphasis on the need to equalise social and economic powers in the name of freedom, but the price of doing so is often violence to those political and civil rights which are just as important to the concept of freedom.

Is it inevitable that a socialist society should commit the mirror-image of the errors which disfigure capitalist society? Or is it possible to achieve the socialist goal of greater freedom and equality without jeopardising the civil and political liberties which are undoubtedly well established in the society we wish to replace? Much depends, in answering these questions, on what we mean by socialism, and it is to that question that we now turn.

3 Socialism

THE CASE AGAINST SOCIALISM

The opponents of socialism argue that, admirable though many socialist objectives may be, they inevitably involve the suppression of individual rights and freedoms. In their quest for equality, socialists necessarily have to restrain those individuals who would otherwise rise above the average and who would demand and obtain more than an equal share of society's benefits. To the extent that a socialist society sets out to redistribute income, wealth and economic power, it must inevitably be confiscatory in respect of those from whom it takes. While the aim may be the commendable one of protecting some individuals against exploitation or discrimination by others, the worthiness of the motivation, it is said, does not make the limitation of freedom any less real or damaging.

Socialists, it is argued, restrict the freedoms not only of those who would otherwise obtain privileges as against others; they also exact a price in terms of lost freedoms from those they seek to protect. This is because, in addition to the offensive action taken against privileged individuals, socialists will also take defensive action, by trying to match the overwhelming strength of some powerful individuals, such as employers and capitalists, with the collective strength of the less powerful.

Collective action may be justified as a rational response to the power of others; but it requires those who participate to recognise the primacy of the collective interest. Unity and solidarity are the key elements in any successful collective action. There is no room for the expression of individual interests within the collective. Any such tendency would mean a fragmentation of the one real strength of the collective – its unity – and would quickly be exploited by those whom the collective was formed to oppose. Socialism, so the argument runs, must therefore not only restrict those whom it opposes, but must also submerge through collective action the individual interests of those who must be protected.

There are other respects, it is said, in which socialism will inevitably limit freedom. In removing the prime motive power in the economy from the hands of the private capitalist, socialists must provide another mainspring for economic activity. To the extent that this mainspring is provided by seeking a more rational use of resources, socialist economies require planning; and if the disposition of economic factors is to be planned, by what reasoning can the disposition of labour be excluded from the ambit of the plan?

In other words, it is implicit in a socialist organisation of the economy that labour should be controlled and directed in accordance with the plan and with the most rational utilisation of resources; and if labour is directed, how can the individual retain any freedom of choice as to where he will work, for whom and in what conditions? And since almost every other aspect of an individual's life – where he lives, where his children go to school and so on – are affected by the question of where he works, does not direction of labour require the complete subjection of the individual to the requirements of the economic plan?

Moreover, if the profit motive is no longer the mainspring of economic activity, some other motivation must be provided. But whereas the drive for profit and for self-improvement clearly originates within the individual, it is by no means so clear that the individual can be relied upon to find within himself the altruism and the concern for the wider community which a socialist society would require. The frailty of the individual in this respect would have to be buttressed by the encouragement, exhortation and even indoctrination provided by the community; and does this not inevitably lead to the regulation of beliefs and ideas, and to the rewarding of those which obtain the community's approval and the discouragement of those which do not?

And if the object of a socialist organisation of society is to place the control of economic activity in the community's, rather than in private hands, and if the community is to be source of motivation and the arbiter of what is acceptable or not, does it not become a question of crucial importance to ask, who is the community? Is not the answer, inevitably, those who also exercise political power? In other words, is it not necessarily true of a socialist society that economic power, with all its immense ramifications, is placed in the hands of the very people who also wield the power of the state?

Instead of the diffusion of power, or at the very least, the dichotomy of power between the capitalist and the politician, does not socialism mean therefore the concentration of power in its fullest sense in a very few hands? Even the greatest possible degree of participation and accountability will provide a safeguard to the individual only in the most formal sense, particularly where the prevailing ethos is the superiority of the collective.

The individual will therefore find himself confronted by a monopoly employer and, to the extent that planning means the restriction or abolition of the free market, a monopoly supplier. He no longer has the choice between one employer and another or one supplier and another. Because it is assumed that in a socialist society he will not be able to set himself up in business, he will have no escape route through self-employment; he must inevitably be someone who is acted upon by economic forces over which he has little control rather than, potentially at least, an actor and an innovator.

Even the positive virtues of socialism, it is argued, contain within themselves the seeds of repression. In encouraging the notion of a community responsibility for the provision of many of the basic requirements of a civilised existence, and in seeking to replace a damaging and wasteful competition with a more rational and efficient co-operation, does not socialism deal a death blow to the concept of individual responsibility and self-reliance, and devalue the importance of individual effort which has been the main progenitor of social advance and the main bulwark against repression?

The critics of socialism furthermore maintain that it is implicit in socialist theory (whether of the utopian or scientific variety) that in a socialist society conflict will cease to exist, either through the altruism of a society purged of the selfishness inherent in the pursuit of individual interest or through the elimination of all class differences following the complete victory of the working class; and that in either case, it is only a short step to the assumption that, to achieve conformity with theory, conflict not only should not but *shall* not exist.

Finally, attention is often drawn to the fact that socialism is, in the eyes of many of its proponents, a social state which can be achieved only through revolution. A justification for the use of force in achieving socialism is easily extended to the defence of socialism once achieved and therefore means, according to the critics, that socialism inevitably gives rise to repressive regimes.

These charges, if accurate, constitute a powerful indictment, sufficient to shake the commitment of all but the most zealous. The accuracy of the indictment, though, depends substantially on whether or not the society attacked by the critics of socialism is indeed socialist.

The targets they have in mind are regimes which do indeed claim to be socialist. They are societies where the state and Party are all-powerful, where those civil and political liberties which are prized in Western liberal democracies are substantially absent, where private property has largely been abolished, and where the economy is centrally owned, planned and directed.

Such societies are indeed vulnerable to attack on libertarian grounds, though their critics, even so, probably do not give them sufficient credit for some of their other achievements. There is no reason, however, why a British socialist should try to defend (and thereby implicitly adopt) these forms of society which are quite alien to most of the traditions of British socialism. There is no reason, in other words, why we should embrace a form of socialism which so conveniently accommodates the prejudices of our opponents.

A modern British socialist should argue, on the contrary, that a fully developed socialism in a Western liberal democracy need not – indeed cannot – display those features which are so easily attacked by critics from the Right. Only intellectual laziness should lead anyone – let alone a socialist – to suppose that a philosophy which begins with such a noble impulse must inevitably lead to such a distorted outcome.

THE DIVERSITY OF SOCIALIST THOUGHT

There is no universally accepted definition of socialism. There are no tablets of stone to be consulted. There is, accordingly, no reason why those who see themselves as socialists should concede to anyone, however eminent, a claim to speak with the one authentic voice of socialism.

This is not to say that the term has no meaning. There is a substantial and recognisable corpus of socialist writing. Writers, thinkers, politicians, labour leaders, who claim to be socialists (and even some who do not) may be said to share certain values and beliefs which are recognisably or at least arguably socialist.

There are some writers, like Marx, whose place in the socialist canon is undisputed. They are often so pre-eminent that they have established their own schools of followers. Their views and arguments are much more easily susceptible to rigorous analysis, discussion and development than the more tenuous concepts of socialism in general. Their teachings often make a special appeal, not just because of their substantive merits, but also because they offer a degree of certainty to those whose temperaments lead them to prefer to work within defined boundaries.

Marx, in particular, offers his followers an intellectual structure of astonishing coherence and comprehensiveness. He is very far, however, from providing a complete blueprint for a modern socialist society and it is unrealistic to seek any one writer who can do so. To expect prescience of that quality and accuracy from writers who were working decades and centuries ago in societies very different from our own is to impose a quite unfair burden on even the most brilliant and eminent. Marx is a towering influence on much modern, and particularly socialist, thought; but he had no supernatural powers.

The best we can hope to do, if we do not subscribe to the teachings of a particular writer but nevertheless wish to bring ourselves within the socialist canon, is to identify those aspects of political thinking which are often found in writers and thinkers who claim to be or are recognised as socialists. Even then, we are faced with difficulties, since many writers who are universally accepted as socialists have advanced views which are directly contradicted by other writers with equally compelling socialist credentials.

A brief analysis of socialist thought will reveal a number of broad themes and different approaches. Many early socialists (including some who would not recognise the term) were utopians; they identified the defects in the social organisation of their time and argued that these arose because society encouraged man's greed and selfishness rather than consciously reflecting in social organisations the greater value of his compassion, tolerance and altruism. Writers of this type placed great emphasis on the need to liberate man from his defects and to educate him to an awareness of the advantages of co-operation.

Many writers in this tradition have been British – from Thomas More to Robert Owen (though Oscar Wilde argued interestingly that one of the great virtues of socialism was that it would liberate people from the need to be altruistic) – but many of the earlier Continental writers, particularly the French, also showed a strong interest in utopian ideas.

A decisive break with this tradition came with the scientific socialists, of whom Marx was the leading example. They argued that socialism was inevitably the next and final stage of social evolution; that it was essentially a matter of economic laws and class interests; and that these factors would necessarily so raise the class consciousness of the most oppressed and numerous class that they would seize power from their oppressors and eventually establish a classless state.

This dichotomy between utopian and scientific socialists falls far short of exhausting the immense diversity of socialist writers, ranging from the virtual anarchy of Godwin to the authoritarianism of Proudhon, and from the philanthropy of Fourier to the ruthlessness of Lenin. For a British reader, there is of course great interest in socialist writers in the specifically British tradition. It is a tradition which has tended to become overshadowed in recent years by the immense achievement of Marx and the diligent scholarship of his disciples. But British socialism, or something very much like it, has a long and distinctive history – from the Putney debates and the Diggers, through Gray, Godwin, non-conformism, Robert Owen, the Chartists, William Morris, the Christian Socialists, the Fabians, Tawney, Cole, Crosland and the modern Marxists. It is only recently that that tradition has owed much to Marx and the scientific socialists.

Of course, British socialists have themselves shown an immense diversity, but it is possible to identify some elements of their thought which are characteristic of a distinctively British, as opposed to a Continental, approach. British socialists have tended to be as interested in political and social arrangements as they are in economics, and they have usually argued for socialism on the basis of its intrinsic merits rather than its historical inevitability. They have often placed emphasis on the ethical aspects of their socialism, believing that a socialist society would be fairer and more equal, as well as more rational and efficient.

Implicit in this approach has been an awareness that in a mature and conservative democracy, it is necessary to win support for socialism; that rational argument and appeals to self-interest are the most promising weapons; that successful revolution is unlikely; and that gradual and constitutional change is the means of achieving socialism most likely to appeal to the British people. A modern writer on socialism in Britain would do well to take account of these conclusions.

THE ELEMENTS OF SOCIALISM

One of the most commonly encountered and seminal ideas to be found among socialist writers is the need to counteract the injustice arising from inequalities in the distribution of economic and political power. The terms in which this idea is expressed will vary according to the precise circumstances with which a particular writer is confronted; but common to many of them is the notion that a socialist must oppose and counteract concentrations of power wherever they may occur, so that power can be diffused as widely as possible.

It is for this reason that most socialists oppose capitalism. A capitalist society is one which not only tolerates the accumulation by some individuals of economic power, but which encourages and depends upon the exploitation of that economic power in order to subjugate others. It is because it has this characteristic – prominently, though not uniquely – that capitalist society is often seen as the antithesis of socialism; there are, however, other forms of society – feudalism or corporatism, for example – which must be regarded as almost equally anti-socialist, and for the same basic reason.

Some socialists, like Marx, do of course regard capitalism as more than just one of a number of possible targets for socialist reform; for Marxists, capitalism is virtually the *raison d'être* of socialism, since they identify capitalism as the necessary precursor of socialism in an inevitable evolutionary process. But socialism is surely more than the automatic heir to capitalism. It must be possible to identify and assert socialist principles and values whether or not capitalism had ever existed. They must have a universal validity, irrespective of time and place and what went before.

Even for Marxists, however, it is arguable that their opposition to capitalism is an expression of a wider principle – of opposition to concentrations of power which threaten ideas of justice and equality and of support for the diffusion of power – and to whose application capitalism is seen as a major obstacle.

Most socialists, even of the non-Marxist variety, have supported the idea of the dignity of labour for the same reasons. There are those – some far from being socialists – who have glorified work as being intrinsically valuable in itself, as a means of self-fulfilment for the individual; in some of these cases, there is a suspicion that the work thus eulogised is more the creative work of the artist than the humdrum work of a factory hand.

But beyond this school of thought, the proper evaluation of labour has been important for socialists as a means of redressing the imbalance between the value placed by society on the contribution made by those who are powerful (and who have economic and political power and social status and privilege to support them) and the contribution made by others who have no power and whose only economic capacity lies in the labour they have to offer.

While it may be true and inevitable for this reason that socialism should find its most natural supporters and beneficiaries among the working class and those who, particularly in industrial societies, work in industry, this cannot be a universal condition of socialism in action. This is because there are societies less advanced than others which have not yet developed, and might never develop, an industrial proletariat, and – even more compellingly in our own case – there may be societies yet to come where manual labour in industry ceases to be a significant part of the wealth-creating process.

This is a development we shall return to later; but for our present purposes it is sufficient to say that a socialism which was limited to expressing the interests of a particular class, involved in a particular form of economic activity, in a particular form of society at a particular stage in its economic development, could be of no more than passing interest. Socialism must have a validity which transcends the particular structures of a given society. The reason that socialism is often identified with the interests of a particular class is that it is that class which is disadvantaged; it is the removal of that disadvantage, whomsoever it affects, and not the promotion of the interests of a particular class, which is the true business of socialism.

Many socialists – perhaps most famously, Proudhon – have argued that private property is at the heart of the social ills which socialists should seek to cure. It is the ownership of property, they argue, which encourages greed and selfishness, which makes possible the accumulation of material goods for some and the deprivation of others, and which in the end creates the imbalance in economic power which allows some members of society to exploit others.

The private property which these socialist reformers had primarily in mind was land. At the time when most of them were writing, land was the one kind of property which really mattered. When Proudhon and others levelled their strictures at private property, they were not attacking the peasant's ownership of a few sticks of furniture, or the artisan's ownership of his tools. It was property which had some economic significance beyond its capacity to serve the personal needs of its owner with which they were concerned.

The landlord and the rentier were accordingly the particular targets of socialist critics. Land was the form of property whose exclusive private ownership could least easily be justified. The title to land rested not on creation but on seizure. The legal system which then protected such claims was simply a manifestation of the power which the ownership of land conferred. It was through such ownership that landowners were able to obtain an unearned income and to use that income to increase their economic advantage. It was rent which impoverished the landless and enriched the landowner.

With the coming of the industrial age, the emphasis of the socialist attack on private property changed, though the problem of land remained unresolved. New industrial development proved an immense generator of wealth; but it also required substantial investment capital. The only people who had the necessary money were the landowners and the merchants; and it was they who accordingly took control of the new wealth-producing process. The unique importance of land as a generator of surplus value was replaced by a multi-faceted commercial, financial and industrial economy which nevertheless shared with land the characteristic that it was privately owned.

Again, however, it was not every form of private property which, in general, drew fire from socialist writers. Property for one's own use or enjoyment was not the target; it was the private ownership of property which had an external economic significance, in the sense that it allowed the owner to accumulate further economic power, which was seen as objectionable. The socialist answer to this problem was public or common or social or co-operative ownership of those forms of property which were important to the wealth-producing process.

The precise form of public ownership (used here in its non-specific sense as the broad antithesis of private ownership) varied according to the preferences of a particular writer or the circumstances obtaining in a particular society. But the broad theme of all such prescriptions was that private property was the institution which allowed the concentration of economic power; some form of public ownership would help to diffuse that power more widely.

The public ownership of the wealth-creating process had further consequences for socialist thought. Without private ownership of the wealth-creating instruments, the drive to obtain private profit and for private aggrandisement could no longer be relied upon to provide the motivation for economic activity, nor could it provide a means of deciding economic priorities or allocating scarce resources. Other motivations and other criteria for decision-making had to be found.

The socialist attack on the concentration of economic power and economic injustice was therefore widened, in the thinking of many socialists, to embrace positive ideas of co-operation (to displace competition), rational planning of economic resources and the acceptance of a community responsibility for the provision of the basic elements of a civilised life.

Many socialist writers believed that the attack on private property (in its economically significant sense) and on private profit-taking called the institutions of the price mechanism and the market into question. For these writers, planning and co-operation could extend well beyond the major issues of macro-economic policy and could decide even very detailed questions which the individual would, under a market system, decide for himself.

A totally planned, rational and co-operative society was often seen by socialist thinkers (understandably enough) as an idealised goal rather than as something which could be immediately achieved. In the meantime, socialists were faced with the hard practical problems of dealing with society as it was and of countering the immense power of those, like the capitalist, in whose hands power was concentrated.

The socialist response to this problem was to combine the puny individual strengths of each member of the disadvantaged group and to use their combined strength to confront and control powerful individuals and institutions. This collective effort placed a premium on unity and solidarity; it was reinforced by perceptions of interests and enemies shared in common; and it required of those involved a sacrifice of their individual objectives in favour of the collective goal.

Collectivism was seen by some socialists as merely a transitional phase in the progress towards socialism – a necessary response to a non-socialist society by those creating socialism. But other socialists saw collectivism not just as a temporary response to the overwhelming power of the capitalist but as an end state towards which socialists should work. Scientific socialists saw collective action arising naturally from the triumph of the oppressed class and the elimination of all other classes; utopian socialists believed that individuals in a socialist state would perceive the advantages of co-operation and would voluntarily relinquish their individual demands in favour of the common good. Collective action was seen as replacing the self-seeking of the individual and supplanting greed, intolerance and selfishness by generosity, compassion and tolerance.

Another major theme of socialist thinking, so far as the transitional pre-socialist stage was concerned, was the need to redistribute wealth and income directly through state action, rather than wait for the day when the system itself would automatically produce a socialist distribution. The re-distribution was to be effected through taxation of the wealthy and expenditure by the community on basic services for the less advantaged.

All of this – the planning of economic resources, the redistribution of wealth, the provision by the community of services, the public ownership of wealth-producing property – meant according to many socialist writers a much increased role for the state. The state would be the only institution large enough, powerful enough and representative enough to undertake the important functions which would be required of collective agencies under a socialist organisation of society. In addition to the traditional functions of defence and internal order, a socialist state would therefore become the prime agency for economic organisation and for the definition and provision of social and political rights.

Marxists have sometimes laid emphasis on Marx's famous reference to the 'withering away of the state' under socialism, but it seems doubtful whether this was an idea which assumed great importance in Marx's own thinking. It was of course consistent with his view that, under socialism, the triumph of the proletariat would eliminate all class conflict and would mean that the state would inevitably serve the interests of the whole society; but this comfortable assumption falls far short of asserting that the mechanisms of the state would have no role to play.

It seems more likely that Marx, in common with many other socialists, paid little attention to the actual organisation of society once the socialist millenium had arrived. Accordingly, writers in this tradition have tended to assume, on the basis of the theoretical identity of interest between each individual and the state, that individual rights in the civil and political sphere did not need separate identification or protection. Other socialists, however, have seen political democracy and the protection of civil rights as the necessary concomitants of the diffusion of economic power.

Underlying much socialist thinking is the belief that man is, if not perfectable, at least open to persuasion and education, and that in socialism he will see a more rational and civilised way of arranging his affairs. There is also the belief that the efforts of individual people, however well-intentioned, are unlikely to redress the balance of injustice, and that a combined effort to change the social system is the only way of achieving greater social justice.

If these are the main themes of socialist thought – a more

equal distribution of economic power, the dignity of labour, public ownership of wealth-producing property, economic planning, co-operation, community responsibility, collective action, a powerful state, the practicability of improving the human condition through social organisation – it is far from clear and it does not necessarily follow that every one of these themes or any combination of them would necessarily produce in practice the sort of society which would commend itself to the modern British socialist.

Are we not obliged to attempt the task of examining the relative weight and value of these ideas and their relevance and acceptability in modern British society? Should we not look behind the labels to see whether these ideas retain their appeal to those who would claim to be socialists? And should we not discriminate between those various forms of society which claim to be socialist and subject them to a rigorous test of their loyalty to the basic objectives of socialist reform?

DISTORTIONS OF SOCIALISM

The truth is that many changes carried out in the name of socialism have betrayed the ideals of socialists. We should not be deterred by the fact that these mistakes have been made and that distortions have occurred; but each such mistake and distortion makes it even more important that we should re-examine our socialism to see how and why it has happened. In particular, we should be prepared to identify those forms of society which, despite their socialist pretensions, are either only partly and imperfectly socialist or represent a complete negation of socialist principles.

Perhaps the most common distortion of socialism in practice is what is often called state capitalism. If we begin with a society in which private capital is dominant and labour is under-valued and exploited, we can try to change this in at least two quite different ways. We can replace the private capitalist with public capital, but in other respects leave the relative positions of capital and labour unchanged; or we can increase the value and importance of the contribution of labour and reduce that of capital.

The former course would not change the essentially capitalist nature of society; and, by entrusting the capitalist role to the state or its agencies, it would in many respects exacerbate the problems which the capital-less experience in relation to the owners and controllers of capital. The power of the capitalist would be reinforced by the monopoly political and economic power exercised by the state in other respects.

The worker, faced with an even more powerful capitalist, would find that his own power to resist and assert himself had been reduced. The difficulties faced by Polish workers in establishing for themselves the independent trade unions which are, rightly, highly valued in the West, illustrates this point. At the extreme, as in China during the 1970s, the worker finds that he is directed where, when and in what conditions he should provide his labour and that he has no choice but to obey. Even the limited element of choice as between one capitalist employer and another which he is permitted by private capitalist organisation is denied to him. The state is, in other words, a more efficient and powerful exploiter of labour than the private owner of capital could ever hope to be. State ownership – nationalisation – can often be just another means of giving priority to the claims of capital and of subjugating the worker.

It may be argued that, unlike the private capitalist, the state capitalist is at least subject to political control and that because the worker has a democratic right to share in that process of control, he can be guaranteed against exploitation. The difficulty here is that political power, even in the most democratic, accountable and representative systems, is in the end exercised by individuals, and that if, in addition to the political power which they exercise by virtue of their office, they also have economic power, they may be very hard to bring under control at the instance of a single individual.

This concentration of power becomes immensely more serious if a further perversion of socialism applies at the same time. This is the notion of so-called democratic centralism or, in other words, the pre-eminence of the Party in political affairs. If all power is concentrated in the hands of the state and its agencies, and those agencies are in turn controlled by the Party – even a supposedly socialist Party – we have the very antithesis of socialism, the denial of power to the ordinary citizen.

This danger has been made real in a number of self-proclaimed socialist countries, but in reality it has more to do with revolutionary theory than with socialism. Dictatorship by a Party elite is not peculiar to regimes claiming to be socialist; and there is no necessary or even clear connection between this view of Party dominance and any of the principles of socialism.

So far as the doctrine of the elite or vanguard Party has any justification, it has more relevance to the so-called pre-revolutionary situation obtaining in Western democracies than it has to societies where socialism has supposedly been achieved. This is because the vanguard Party has a clear role, in some revolutionary theory, in bringing about the revolution by which it is supposed that socialism will be ushered in. The Party élite must, according to this theory, raise the political consciousness of the proletariat, not by revealing to them the full scope of the socialist revolution which is planned, but by engaging their support in lesser struggles. The doctrine means in effect a deliberate conspiracy by a self-appointed élite against the very people they are supposed to help and reveals a profound contempt for the ordinary citizen.

The danger for the Labour Party, or any democratic socialist Party, if such a doctrine prevailed, is clear. The doctrine might just about make sense (though it would still be profoundly un-socialist in its implications) if there were a realistic prospect of the working class being led unwittingly to revolution; but since the only realistic course for bringing about socialist change in a modern democracy is through popular support, the concept of a vanguard Party is a positive obstacle to that aim. The wider electorate do not take long to perceive that a Party is more concerned with its own élite than with obtaining popular support.

Even in the unlikely case that this approach could be justified in terms of some practical strategy for achieving power, it still could not be justified in even the remotest sense as a means of achieving socialism. This is because the establishment of a vanguard or élite Party denies the basic objective of socialism – the diffusion of power and the greatest possible degree of equality and freedom for the individual.

The essence of socialism does not lie in the vesting of all power in the state or in domination by the Party. The concentration of power in a few hands and the reduction of the individual's control over his own life are both distortions of the socialist ideal. Nor does socialism imply any restriction of political democracy or diminution of civil and political liberties, which are often seen as the necessary concomitants of the pre-eminence of state and Party; if and when these things are done in the name of socialism they betray a complete ignorance of the wider aims of socialist society.

Many distortions of socialism occur because of an overly theoreticaly and ideological attachment to some limited practical goal. Private property is usually identified as one of the principal institutions of capitalism; yet it is perfectly possible for socialism to be established without taking all property into public ownership. If the true socialist objective of diffusing economic power is kept in mind, then a more flexible approach to the question of private property is possible and is more likely to achieve both popular support and a truly socialist objective.

The private ownership of one's home and of possessions which are for personal enjoyment can indeed be seen as important means of extending the freedom of the individual and of insulating him against the pretensions and powers of external agencies – both legitimate socialist objectives. The point at which a socialist would limit private property rights is when they cease to be a matter of personal enjoyment and protection against the power of others and become instead instruments of economic power and economic aggression against others. It is at this point that the socialist demands, in conformity with the wider socialist objectives, that property should be brought under proper social control.

Similarly, the socialist need not, as he is too often urged to do, reject all the workings of the market. It is when the market becomes a mechanism for exploiting the less powerful, for making possible the accumulation of economic power in a few hands and for making economic decisions according to the limited criteria of maximising profits for a few, that the socialist will wish to intervene, and to make sure that checks, controls and other criteria are introduced and have proper effect. The socialist will also regard the market as seriously defective as a means of providing those social goods – like a healthy environment or a system for reducing accidents at work – which require collective decision and action.

It will also be inappropriate as a means of making strategic decisions for the economy and society; it is too arbitrary and capricious, and takes too short-term a view, to have entrusted to it those wider issues which involve more than simple questions of profit and loss, supply and demand. Those tasks are best undertaken by those whose horizons are not limited by such short-term considerations.

Yet the market remains a substantially more efficient means of allocating resources at the level of the micro-economy than any bureaucratically controlled system of planning and rationing. It also provides the individual worker *qua* consumer with some element of control and choice over the disposition of his own economic power – and certainly a greater degree of choice and control than he would enjoy under a totally planned system.

At this level, therefore, the market is substantially consistent with the wider socialist objective of spreading economic power and maximising the range of choice available to the least economically powerful individual. There is nothing intrinsically objectionable to socialists about markets, which could, of course, operate in principle without depending on the private ownership of capital. It is possible to conceive of a market operating in the public interest rather than for private gain, providing a mechanism for deciding consumer preferences and fulfilling what Rawls calls (*A Theory of Justice*, p. 273) an allocative rather than a distributive function.

It is the failure to identify the point at which social institutions and mechanisms become anti-social which lies at the heart of the failure of much socialist analysis. The social arrangement whose initial purpose and effect is beneficial in socialist terms but which has, if unchecked, a tendency to reinforce itself cumulatively so as to become oppressive is a common phenomenon; the problem of deciding when and how that arrangement should be checked, so as to preserve its benefits but limit its abuses, is one to which socialists must pay special attention.

Too many socialists identify social arrangements which, unchecked, give rise to abuses, and conclude that those social arrangements are intrinsically objectionable and must be abolished altogether, without regard for the beneficial social (and socialist) purposes which those arrangements can serve. There is of course an admirable radicalism which underlies much of the socialist analysis – the notion that only the most root and branch reform will suffice to remove injustice. Yet this instinct for total abolition and replacement, rather than control and reform, is among the most treacherous of socialist habits of thought.

There is no reason why socialism should mean the complete antithesis of every aspect of our present society. There is much we have achieved that, with some modification and in the context of a wider socialist reform, can serve a socialist purpose. For the socialist, as for any other social reformer, the intensity of the desire for change is no substitute for proper analysis or the exercise of judgment in matters where drawing lines is not always easy or clear-cut.

This is not, however, a plea for doing less than is necessary to bring about a socialist reform. Palliatives can never bring about socialism. The notion that, for example, the redistribution of wealth, or the creation of a welfare state, are all that is needed to achieve socialism is to misunderstand and under-value the essential socialist belief that it is the social arrangements themselves, and not just their consequences, which have to be changed.

Fundamental changes in the power relationships and structures in society are necessary, so that society itself is set on a course which inevitably reflects and creates socialist values. This is not to say that the redistribution of wealth or the welfare state are not valuable adjuncts to a socialist re-organisation; but they are not in themselves a sufficient condition of socialism.

THE ESSENCE OF SOCIALISM

What then is the essential idea of socialism – common to all or most socialist writers – and which retains its validity and relevance when applied to modern conditions? What is the concept of socialism towards which socialists in modern Britain should be working?

A socialist, as the term itself implies, places great value on the role of man *in society* – as a social creature. The socialist welcomes and values the immense benefits which accrue to the individual from his social relations with others; but he will also recognise that in all societies there are inherent tendencies which inevitably lead, unless checked, to dangers and abuses.

The individual in society inevitably yields to others, in return for the benefits he receives, some degree of control over his own life. This process of deriving benefits and yielding power is not a once-for-all and static event; it is dynamic, constantly being re-defined and changed. The adjustments which are constantly made bring into being both concentrations and deficiencies of power. The changes in those power relationships have their own momentum and inevitably reinforce themselves over time. There is, in other words, a natural tendency towards the accumulation of power by those who are more powerful and for the increasing loss of power (or freedom) by those who already have less.

The response made to this dynamic and natural social process of the concentration of power is at the heart of the issues to be resolved by political philosophy. It is here that the socialist position must and does distinguish itself from other political attitudes.

The *laissez-faire* liberal (now finding his main political expression in the Thatcherite Tory Party) regards the cumulative process towards the unequal distribution of power and freedom as, if not actually desirable, the inevitable and worthwhile price to be paid for the full exercise of individual freedom. He welcomes the dynamism of the process as the best and only guarantor of progress, even if there are inevitably casualties on the way. Any interference with this process can only be, from this viewpoint, at the expense of individual freedom and social progress. We saw in an earlier chapter, however, that this approach is severely deficient and self-defeating, even from the viewpoint of those who prize individual freedom above all other values.

The traditional conservative is equally convinced that a concentration of power must occur in society, but he is less happy to accept the dynamism of the process. He believes that society derives great benefits not only from the accumulation of power by a small minority but also from the assurance that that advantage should be maintained in the same hands over a long period. His emphasis is therefore on the preservation of the status quo. He attempts to mitigate its harshness and unfairness by imposing an element of social stability, based on respect for authority and tradition, by an acceptance of a hierarchical social system and by the recognition by those who enjoy privilege of at least a rudimentary obligation to protect those who are less advantaged.

It is a little more difficult to identify the response which might be made by the newly emerging centrist group in British politics – the modern Liberals and the Social Democrats – mainly because their ideas remain pretty nebulous. But, as we shall see later, it seems likely that, like the conservatives, they will accept the inevitability and beneficence of concentrations of power; they will seek to mitigate the damaging effects by establishing an equality of opportunity.

The socialist, on the other hand, deliberately seeks to establish a social system which, while preserving the very real benefits of social co-operation, operates to prevent and counteract the concentration of power which poses such a huge threat to individual liberty. It is this attack on the concentration of power, and the diffusion and equalisation of power among all members of society, which is the essence of socialism. This objective requires detailed attention to the actual institutions and mechanisms by which it is to be achieved.

What are those institutions and mechanisms? It is not the purpose of this study to describe fully the detail of a socialist organisation of society, but rather to indicate a form of socialism which is true to the wider aims of socialist reform and which is compatible with the concept of individual freedom. Nevertheless, the argument here advanced, that socialism is essentially a corrective mechanism designed to prevent and counteract the tendency towards the concentration of power, needs to be fleshed out with some concrete examples, in order to aid a full understanding of what is proposed.

Many of the mechanisms by which socialism will operate will be those with which we are already familiar. There are of course many self-proclaimed socialists for whom the very fact that an institution or mechanism already exists in our society is all that is needed to show that it cannot be socialist. It is certainly true that it is quintessentially socialist always to look forward, and to refuse to accept that the status quo is acceptable or the best that can be achieved, and this for the very good reason that as society changes and develops so the socialist response must also change and develop. We can never say that socialism has been achieved, because socialism is not an end-state; it is rather a process which must constantly be applied and adapted to a society which has an inherent and infinitely varied tendency to move away from the socialist ideal.

Yet we should be foolish to accept the naive view that nothing already achieved can be socialist. To do so would be to devalue the immense advances which have been made by socialist reformers in the past, to discourage current socialists by implying that the achievement of any real socialist advance must constantly be deferred to some never-to-be-realised future, and to lose sight of a valuable and readily accessible insight into the contemporary meaning and potential of socialism.

The absence of any widely accepted and currently relevant theory of socialism is therefore a handicap, not only in terms of planning for future socialist action, but also in terms of understanding and providing a satisfactory theoretical explanation of what has already been achieved in the name of socialism. We should therefore be suspicious of any theory of socialism that fails to encompass, explain and properly value the socialist progress already made.

SOCIALIST ACHIEVEMENTS

The first and essential element of a socialist society is undoubtedly political democracy – the power which is shared and exercised by every adult citizen to vote in and, even more importantly, to vote out the government of the country. It is fashionable in some quarters to emphasise the limitations of this power; and it is true that a single vote cast at irregular intervals of some years is far from being a comprehensive or sufficient instrument of political democracy. But it is not necessary to claim more for it than what it is worth. That worth can best be measured by considering the consequences of its absence. A person denied the right to vote would rightly feel that he had been deprived of the most fundamental means by which to make his contribution to the joint enterprise of society and to the protection of his own individual status within society.

The view that democracy is of value is of course widely held by many people across the political spectrum. Why, then, can socialists lay special claim to it as an essential part of their political philosophy? The answer is not just that socialists have been in the forefront of the battle to secure political democracy and that the struggles to secure socialism and democracy have gone hand in hand. The reason that they have been inseparable, for most of those who fought for them, is that political democracy is a manifestation in the political sphere of the principles that socialists wish to extend throughout society.

Democracy is, in other words, the basic political expression of the socialist view that power must be diffused and that everyone must have the maximum degree of political power commensurate with a similar power exercised by others. It is no accident that, as ordinary people were enfranchised for the first time and were able to exercise political power, they created the Labour Party as their instrument, and that socialism is widely and rightly viewed as a doctrine which serves the interests of the ordinary man or woman.

That is why those so-called socialists who deny or devalue the importance of democracy fail to understand the true nature and objectives of socialism. The same point can be made in relation to other aspects of civil and political liberties. The limitation of civil rights – the right to express dissenting opinions, join organisations, move about freely, and so on – can never be compatible with the socialist aim of maximising the individual's control over his own life; on the contrary, the widest possible extension of such rights is the only truly socialist objective.

Some socialists in Britain, while agreeing that democracy is an essential aspect of socialism, nevertheless take a more jaundiced view of the rule of law. They are inclined to view the law and the judicial system as institutions which serve the interests of those who exercise power, and there is undoubtedly some justice in this view. The point can be made most clearly in relation to the traditional care and ingenuity shown by the common law in the protection of private property rights, by contrast with the scant regard paid to the rights of employees.

Nevertheless, the rule of law is important to socialists. The law itself may, in its content and substance, reflect the disposition of power in society, but the principle that all are, in procedural terms, equal before the law, and that no one – neither king nor bureaucrat – is above the law is a guarantee of particular value to socialists. This is because equality before the law and universal subordination to it are effective safeguards against the abuse of power. The socialist must always aim at an ideal society in which power is equally shared by all; but in the real world, despite the application of socialist principles, power will be held unequally, and the rule of law will provide a safeguard for those less powerful and open to exploitation.

The law is important, not only as an instrument for protecting the individual against exploitation, but also as a means of counteracting discrimination against members of groups. Racist or sexist discrimination is a fundamental denial of the socialist concern for the rights and dignity of each individual in society. The law has an important part to play as a statement of society's principles and as a shaper of social attitudes. Statutory anti-discrimination measures, although far from complete (especially in the case of discrimination against women), are an inescapable obligation for the socialist.

There are other aspects of current British society which can claim to be socialist mechanisms for correcting imbalances of power. An obvious example is redistributive taxation, as is the use of the tax revenues so raised to provide public services of special value (in principle, if not always in practice) to the less privileged. The community's acceptance of the responsibility for providing the basics of life, including health, education, food and shelter, is the expression of an essentially socialist concept. A realistic assessment of the practical efficacy of such measures should not blind us to the socialist nature of the impulse which produces them.

Socialists have brought about other changes in society. The fact that these changes have not yet gone far enough need not preclude us from drawing attention to them. The market is no longer unfettered in its operations. The consumer is protected in a variety of ways against exploitation. The seeker after private profit is increasingly made, through laws against pollution and for the protection of the environment, to bear the social as well as the balance-sheet cost of his activities. The worker is given protection against his employer, in terms of job security, trade union rights, terms and conditions, and health and safety. His job is increasingly regarded as a piece of property which is afforded, through provisions governing notice, unfair dismissal and redundancy payments, the kind of protection hitherto reserved for property.

The rights of property owners themselves, and particularly their rights to accumulate property, have been limited by taxation, by rules against the accumulation and the disposition of property in perpetuity, and by the planning legislation. Increasingly, the social case for economic activity is recognised. The community accepts an increasing responsibility for stimulating economic activity, through public financing, through public training schemes, through the public allocation of scarce resources and through macro-economic planning.

Each of these measures or developments is properly to be regarded as socialist in inspiration, because the object of each is the diffusion and equalisation of power and liberty. It is this common feature which stamps each of them as socialist; it is this impulse which is at the heart of socialism.

This is not to say that socialism has already been achieved and that all we have to do is to recognise it. Socialism is not a destination at which we shall arrive one day; there are no final victories in politics. Socialism is a constant struggle against the forces in society which naturally tend towards the concentration of power. Even with substantial achievements behind us, we have much yet to do; and even when we have achieved all those things which can currently be identified as socialist objectives, there will be other, as yet unforeseeable, battles still to be fought.

SOCIALIST TASKS

We are, in other words, far from having brought about a social system which brings into play the automatic corrective mechanisms demanded by socialism. Despite socialist advances, capital remains the pre-eminent element in wealth-creation. The owners of capital – whether private or public, individual or corporate – still own, control and enjoy the fruits of the wealth-producing process and buy and sell working lives as though they were commodities. Economic power is still concentrated in their hands, with the necessary correlative that it is removed from the hands of the bulk of ordinary people for whom the wage bargain remains unequal and demeaning.

The law still provides, through the institution of the joint-stock, limited liability company, enormous privileges to the owners of capital, who are thereby enabled to conduct their business affairs with an irresponsibility which would be totally condemned in the private affairs of the ordinary working man.

Wider share ownership may have diffused ownership to a limited extent but it has not inhibited a major concentration of control.

The law still underpins the whole concept of succession and inheritance, so that private property – essentially an artificial, social concept which needs the backing of the law to protect it – can be accumulated to an extent well beyond that needed to satisfy even the most outrageous appetites for personal consumption. The right of inheritance, which may have been tolerable when a matter of a workman's tools, is less so when it is a question of large fortunes. In the case of land, private ownership means that the value which the community has itself created in land is exploited by some individuals to their benefit but at enormous cost to the community interest.

The concentration of economic power determines the disposition of other forms of power as well. At a time when the power of the press, and more particularly of the electronic media, is becoming more and more significant, the ownership and control of those media is becoming less and less representative, and more and more identified with the narrow interests of the economically powerful. We have reached the point where our so-called free press is in practice accessible only to those with huge financial resources.

It is still possible – indeed, increasingly so – to use economic power to buy educational, vocational, health and social privilege. The community, through its government, is yielding up rather than discharging the responsibility it formerly assumed for the provision of necessary public services. The government is withdrawing from its role as overall director of economic strategy and from its responsibility to maintain full employment. Excessive importance is still given in macro-economic policy to the interests of those who hold assets and deal in money rather than to the interests of those who work for a living by making things in factories.

The welfare state, though valuable and important in itself, remains a palliative for dealing with the casualties of a system which necessarily produces major and self-reinforcing inequalities and injustices. The search for private profit remains the major motivation for economic activity.

Each of these features of present society represents a further challenge to the socialist reformer. Each of them is a manifestation of that natural tendency towards the concentration of power against which the socialist must react. We remain a profoundly unequal society in which the rewards of social co-operation are unfairly distributed in favour of those who control the levers of power.

The challenge is not a static one. In many respects, the nature of modern technological society will exacerbate these trends and increase the socialist task. The replacement of human labour by machines has not yet happened – and indeed may be longer deferred than many currently expect. The whole history of technological advance in this field is one of freeing human labour from the more arduous and repetitive tasks, with the result that the accomplishment of more complex and demanding tasks becomes possible. It may be, therefore, that we are still some distance away from a workless and leisured society, simply because the appetite for new goods and services, including many of which we cannot currently conceive, is virtually infinite.

Nevertheless, the importance of human labour is likely to decline in relation to capital as a factor in creating wealth; and this will create major problems for the socialist. It will no longer be sufficient to extol the virtues of labour, or to organise labour so as to counteract the power of the capitalist, since the balance of economic advantage will have moved inexorably against the worker. Access to capital will become virtually all that matters for wealth-creation; the rights which accompany the ownership of capital will become even more extensive because of the declining claims of those who contribute their labour. Unless some form of social ownership of capital and of the wealth-creating process is introduced, the future for the bulk of the population will be that of powerless and superfluous drones, living on social security handouts provided and fixed by those who own the wealth created by the machines.

Such a future offers both a challenge and an opportunity. It will mean, on the one hand, that there will no longer be a large wage-earning and labouring class who could be regarded as socialism's natural supporters and beneficiaries. Many of those who will be most powerless and who will be most in need of the protection offered by a socialist society will be so precisely because their labour has no economic value and no longer enters into economic calculations about the wealth-creating process.

Labour will be, as a provider of services, more in the nature of a consumer good than an element in wealth creation.

The whole Marxist analysis, in other words, will be threatened by the removal of one of its major premises. Labour will be by-passed rather than exploited; surplus value will no longer be extracted in quite the way that the Marxist analysis explains. But the likely future irrelevance of much of Marxism will not mean that socialism itself is no longer relevant.

Indeed, the socialist analysis will become even more important in a future when technological change and the increasing importance of capital mean that power is potentially concentrated in fewer and fewer hands. A socialist mechanism for diffusing that power and breaking down its concentration will become even more urgent. The case for socialism will become more obvious, and the demand for socialist reform more widespread, when most people are denied even the minimal economic power available to them through the sale of their labour.

There are other aspects of the new technology which will make socialist reform more imperative. Information technology is the area where rapid advances are most likely. The citizen will have available to him, and in many senses will not be able to avoid, an enormously increased and sophisticated volume of information. Every aspect of his life will be influenced by the information he absorbs.

Those who control the sources of that information will be in a position of enormous power. The diversity of free competition will not be a sufficient guarantee against the exploitation of this power, since the capital investment required will mean that access to it is limited to those who are already powerful. The only true safeguard will be a conscious diversification, according to criteria other than those that usually apply in the market place. Some form of social control of information technology will be urgently needed if we are not to develop a society conditioned to conform with the values of that increasingly small minority who wield power.

This, then, is the outlook for the modern socialist. His overriding aim is to maximise the power (and therefore the freedom) exercised by each and every citizen. This can be done only by diffusing power as widely as possible – in other words, by sharing it equally. Because there is a natural tendency in society

towards the concentration of power, the socialist will constantly
devise means of breaking down such concentrations. Because
society is dynamic, infinitely variable and unpredictable in its
development, it is not possible to identity for all times and for all
places the mechanisms and institutions which will serve the
socialist purpose. The complete and permanent equalisation of
power is in any case an unrealisable ideal; all that the socialist
can do is to ensure that corrective mechanisms are in place to
drag society back towards the ideal, and that those mechanisms
can be adapted as necessary and as society itself changes.

Some of these mechanisms are already in place, and are doing
their job effectively. There are other concentrations of power
for which there is not as yet an effective corrective mechanism.
Likely developments in the future make the search for
corrective mechanisms even more urgent and significant, and
reinforce the case for a flexible socialist response in order to
achieve the basic socialist aim of the maximum possible
diffusion of power.

A SOCIALIST SOCIETY

If we envisage a society in which socialist principles are made
applicable and relevant to modern conditions and accordingly
attract popular support, in which socialist achievements are
preserved and extended, and in which the tasks which obviously
remain to challenge the socialist are successfully undertaken,
what would such a society look like?

It would, first and foremost, be a society which placed a much
greater value on, and aimed much more deliberately at, a
fundamental equality of social and economic, as well as
political, power. Political democracy and the proper
safeguarding of civil and political rights would be an essential
part of this equality, but it would also require a much greater
equalisation of the benefits of social co-operation.

The principal means of preventing extremes of wealth and
power from developing would be the greatest possible
attribution to each individual of the power to control his own
life. The essence of socialism would be that this effort would be
made in respect of each individual, and not just those who were

able to grab such power for themselves and at the expense of others.

This would mean the removal of all those social institutions, mechanisms and rules which allowed and encouraged the accumulation, reinforcement and entrenchment of advantage. On this ground, the ownership of capital and its role in the wealth-creating process would have to be brought under social control.

The privileges accorded to the owners of capital, through mechanisms like the joint-stock company (in terms of granting both immunities from ordinary liability and of special rights of ownership and control), would have to be ended. Where capital was supplied by private individuals and institutions, this would be done on terms which allowed a proper return and no more – that is, a proper price would be paid for the capital, in the same way that a proper price is paid for any other commodity.

Capital would, of course, remain essential to wealth-creation, but it would increasingly be supplied (as is happening to some degree in any case) by the community rather than by the private capitalist. Greater attention would be paid to the means by which the savings of ordinary people, which are already the major source of new money for investment, are collected, managed and invested, so that the social ownership which is implicit in the contribution which each individual makes, as taxpayer or as participant in savings and pension schemes, would be given practical meaning.

This would mean that various forms of social or public ownership would become the norm, but it would also require a much greater flexibility than has been evidenced so far in the forms which that ownership might take. State capitalism would no longer be the sole model; the public corporation, which might still be appropriate in a few cases, would be supplemented by municipal enterprises, co-operatives (of both producers and consumers) and by enterprises in which collectively invested savings obtained certain rights for their owners.

Where an individual wished to set himself up in business, it would not be his contribution of capital but the investment of his ideas and effort and his undertaking of obligations in the name of the business which gave him control of his enterprise. As soon as he needed the investment of other people's ideas and energies, however, he could no longer expect to retain sole control and ownership rights. The wage bargain, in other words, which at present subordinates the contributors of labour to the owners of capital would have to be completely re-cast, so that, subject to some minimum requirements as to duration and substance, those who contributed their labour would be regarded by law as joint participants in the enterprise.

None of this need affect the right of the individual to own property for his own private use and consumption. Indeed, the individual's ownership of his own home and of other items for the use and enjoyment of himself and his family would be an important element in giving him control over his own life and providing a bulwark against the claims made on him by other elements in society.

The ownership of private property would, however, be subjected to a number of conditions in order to safeguard the community interest – as is done already, for example, through the planning legislation. As private property rights became more extensive, so as to exceed the needs of personal consumption, the community interest would have to become more predominant. This would be especially true of resources which were of particular importance to the community – especially those which could not be expanded or renewed, and those whose value the community itself had largely created, like land. The community interest in such cases could be protected in a variety of ways, including the payment to the community of some part of the value which the community had created.

These changes would be made as part of the general socialist drive to break down concentrations of power (in these cases, of the economic power currently exercised through the ownership of capital) which threaten equality, social cohesion and individual liberty. They would be supplemented by specific rules to prevent and control the acquisition of monopoly or quasi-monopoly power. Subject to safeguards of this sort, there is no reason why a socialist society should not use the market as the most efficient means of allocating resources and meeting consumer demands in the short term, while reserving wider-ranging strategic decisions about the future course of economic activity to a properly accountable and democratic planning agency.

It is not just the economic power wielded by the capitalist, however, which threatens the principles and values of a socialist society. The socialist would have to be alert to concentrations of other forms of power. As we said earlier, political democracy and the rule of law, guaranteeing civil rights and providing enforceable remedies against the abuse of power, will be essential to protect the individual against the immense power of the state.

There is nothing in the socialism we have so far described which implies a conflict between these safeguards and the other elements of a socialist economic and social organisation. Indeed, a failure to provide them would mean a denial of the basic objectives of socialism.

The individual would also have to be protected against other concentrations of power. It would be pointless so to arrange matters that he was safeguarded against exploitation or abuse by a boss or bureaucrat or policeman, if he were nevertheless left unprotected against those who controlled organisations which he was obliged to join. In the socialist society we envisage, the importance of collective organisations would be much diminished, since the concentrations of power which they were formed to oppose would have been broken down already by socialist reforms, and the individual would no longer need protection against them to the same degree.

Nevertheless, it would still be important to ensure that, where the individual does belong to an organisation which exercises real power, such as a professional body or a trade union, rules enforceable at his instance exist to protect him. To some socialists, the notion that the individual needs protection against his trade union will be anathema; to some extent, this is understandable in the light of the important defensive role which the trade union undertakes on behalf of its members in current society.

It is important to recognise, however, that even in today's circumstances – and the point will be even stronger in a society which reflects socialist values more fully – oppression is oppression wherever it originates. If the socialist is to be taken seriously in his attempt to enlarge the powers of each individual in society, he cannot be seen to be picking and choosing in the concentrations of power he attacks.

The freeing of the individual from the oppressive concentration of power will be central to the socialist organisation of society. The community will at the same time take responsibility for the provision, in a positive sense, of the basic social and economic conditions which each individual needs in order to make the fullest use, if he chooses, of his personal capacities.

This will require the community, through its democratically elected government, to assume the direction of macro-economic policy, with the particular object of making proper use, in the community interest, of the resources available. Full employment, or at least the best possible use of the human resources available to society, will be the central task in this field.

The community will also assume responsibility for guaranteeing to each individual in society access to the basic requirements of life in that society – educational opportunity, health care, decent housing, enough money to live on, special provision for those who are specially disadvantaged, and so on.

In such a society, where community responsibility is important, where oppressive concentrations of power are consciously counteracted, and where each individual is free to develop his own potential if he wishes, socialist values will also be free to flourish. This does not imply in any sense that any attempt at indoctrination need be made. What it does mean, however, is that the ethical and aesthetic values of a given society will reflect the qualities which are rewarded, in terms of success and esteem, by the economic and social arrangements of that society; and that this will be true where those qualities are no longer those of selfishness and greed and the exploitation of others, but arise from the freedom of each individual to realise his own potential in a context where the same freedom for others and the community interest are both guaranteed.

How, then, would such a socialist society meet the charges made, from a libertarian viewpoint, by right-wing critics? It is certainly true that some individuals – those who already had a substantial and perhaps excessive share of society's benefits – would find that their freedom was curtailed; but as we saw in an earlier chapter, it is not possible to conclude from that alone that society as a whole is less free. Indeed, to the extent that that curtailment affected social and economic powers of a less fundamental nature, and was matched in terms of quantity and exceeded in terms of value by a corresponding increase in freedom for others, so that freedom was equalised and therefore maximised, the libertarian attack on this ground seems misplaced.

The subordination of the individual interest to that of some collective body, as a means of counteracting the overwhelming power of some individuals and institutions, would be less necessary in this form of socialism than in our present society, since society as a whole would be organised to protect the individual. And since the individual would be free to own his own property, to choose his own form of work and to make his purchases in a market in which suppliers continued to compete, it could not be said of this socialist society that the individual is inevitably faced with a monopoly employer and supplier.

His freedom to act in the economic sphere would, on the contrary, be greatly enhanced by the equalisation and maximisation of economic and social powers. Moreover, by diffusing both economic and political power, this form of socialism would also provide a defence against the usual charge that, under socialism, the same people would exercise and monopolise all the power that mattered.

It is true that, by emphasising the community's responsibility for guaranteeing certain basic decencies of life to each individual, this socialist society could be said to diminish the individual virtues of self-reliance and enterprise; but this is to reflect an unavoidable clash of values between Right and Left, rather than to make a point which has much to do with freedom. In any case, individual enterprise would be encouraged, rather than discouraged as it is at present for most people, when society was organised to make it possible for everyone to make the best use of his capacities.

Finally, because this form of socialism would seek to establish and maintain itself on the basis of the appeal it made to and the support it gained from the mass of the people, it could not be attacked on the ground that it was in any sense totalitarian. On the contrary, it would represent the fullest possible extension, to every aspect of social life, of the principles of democracy.

CURRENT ISSUES

We may therefore safely assert that a socialist society constructed along these lines would avoid many of the fundamental charges usually made against those societies in Eastern Europe and elsewhere which claim to be socialist but which deny many of the basic socialist principles. There remain, however, a number of issues which arise in contemporary British politics, and which appear to lend substance to the charge that socialist reform inevitably requires some limitation of individual liberty.

Many of these charges are based on little more than political prejudice and an inability on the part of those making them to judge social phenomena objectively. A good example is the antagonism aroused by the supposed role of trade unions. It is often argued, for example, that the post-entry closed shop is a prime example of socialism in action and that it illustrates clearly the extent to which socialism would involve a curtailment of freedom of choice.

In fact, as we suggested earlier, the importance of collective organisations like trade unions would be likely to diminish in a socialist society where each member of society could be guaranteed that society as a whole was organised to meet the interests of all, and not just some, of its members. But, even setting aside as a justification the extent to which the present organisation of society necessitates the formation of collective organisations to defend their members' interests, it is still the case that criticism of the closed shop on libertarian grounds is misplaced.

Because a contract of employment is the basis on which most people are able to work and earn a living, we have become accustomed to, and indeed hardly notice, that the relationship between employer and employee is a coercive one in which the employer still has immense power. While legislation has modified to some extent the traditional right of the employer to hire and fire, it remains the essential characteristic of the employment contract.

The employer has the right to choose whether or not to employ at all, whether to employ this one or that (he could if he wished exclude from his employment all fair-haired people), whether to require his employees to join pension schemes, social clubs and so on, what type of work they should do, what hours they should work and what pay and conditions they should be offered, and in what circumstances and on what conditions their employment should be terminated. What the employer is given under a contract of employment is the right to require other people to do his bidding for a large part of their waking lives.

None of this is regarded with the slightest degree of surprise or concern by most people. It is simply an accepted part of a familiar social and economic landscape. There are very few to protest that these virtually limitless powers of the employer over his employees constitute an important limitation of individual freedom.

Yet, as soon as it is suggested that, in addition to these far-reaching conditions of employment which are solely determined by the employer, there should be one more – a condition not simply imposed by one person but freely negotiated by employer and employees alike – there are howls of protest from so-called libertarians. Those who happily accept conditions of employment determined by their employer, including requirements that they should join pension schemes, holiday clubs, staff associations and so on, suddenly seem to believe that their liberty is threatened because they might also be required to join a trade union.

The suspicion must arise that these protests owe more to anti-trade union prejudice and unfamiliarity with the notion that working people might actually have some say in their working conditions than to any objective analysis of the issues of personal freedom involved. This is not to say that the closed shop does not represent a limitation of freedom of choice, but merely that it is hard to see why, in its operation and purpose, it is any more objectionable than many other constraints which go unremarked. Many anti-socialist objections can be similarly explained in terms of a failure to recognise existing social rules and institutions for what they are, and of an unthinking readiness to condemn the unfamiliar.

Similar considerations apply to the charge that, in a socialist system, people would not be free to spend their money as they wish – a point often made in respect of the threat which Labour Governments are thought to pose to private health care and education. Here, too, it is important to identify clearly the issues at stake.

The Labour Party has so far confined its attack on private health care and education to somewhat marginal issues; in the case of health care, the argument has been about the extent to which profit-seekers should be entitled to use the skills and facilities provided at the public expense, while in the field of education, the debate has centred on the fiscal privileges enjoyed by so-called public schools. These issues are simply those of equity; they do not at first sight seem to raise any question of individual freedom.

It is true that underlying the somewhat jaundiced view which most socialists take of private health care and education is the conviction that it is inappropriate, in a civilised society, that the quality of the health care and educational opportunity available to its citizens should be determined by their purchasing power. In a civilised society – in a socialist society – it is argued that the availability of health care should be determined by need and that educational provision should match the inclinations and abilities of those who benefit from it.

The socialist would also argue that, irrespective of whether it is better or worse, the provision of different levels and types of health care and education according to one's ability to pay for them is likely to be socially divisive; indeed, that in the field of education, it is very often the social exclusivity, rather than a specifically educational advantage, which is being purchased.

But to argue this, and to propose that those special concessions which encourage anti-social practices should be removed, is a far cry from outright prohibition. Yet, even if it were total prohibition of private health care and education which was proposed, the case would not be as clear-cut as so many anti-socialist critics seem to assume.

In contemporary Britain, people are prohibited from spending their money on a variety of purposes which they might like to pursue and are conversely compelled to spend their money on other purposes of which they might disapprove. The restrictions imposed by the criminal and planning laws are examples of the former; the dedication of some part of each taxpayer's tax payment to maintaining our nuclear defence force is an example of the latter. So, the principle that people are compelled to take account of social factors in deciding their pattern of spending is not exactly unknown.

The question of whether spending on private health care and education should join those forms of expenditure which are prohibited in the public interest is not therefore one which necessarily raises issues of fundamental personal liberty. It is essentially a question of degree and judgment. On the one hand, there are those who say that such expenditure is no different from, and no more socially significant than, other forms of private consumption, and that there is therefore no ground for outlawing it. On the other hand, there are those who say that it is socially divisive, unfair and immoral, and therefore as socially harmful as other forms of prohibited behaviour.

In a socialist society animated by a determination to ensure that power is shared and is not concentrated in just a few hands, the answer to these questions will turn on the extent to which the purchase by the already privileged of further educational and health privilege (or even just exclusivity) reinforces their advantage and leads to a cumulative concentration of power in their hands, such as to reduce the power and therefore the freedom of others. The objection which socialists have to fee-paying schools and to private health care is precisely on these grounds.

Much will depend on the level of provision which society makes for those who do not wish or do not have the capacity to purchase these forms of privilege. A society which makes proper provision for all its citizens in these matters would have less to fear from private provision, since it would then be less likely that real questions of power and freedom would arise. In those circumstances, the gap between private and public provision would be marginal; the choice between availing oneself of public provision on the one hand and purchasing private provision on the other would turn on matters of whim and fancy, rather than on the pursuit of privilege.

It is this course of generous public provision which socialists should prefer to the course of prohibition. The essence of that position is the genuinely socialist one of insisting that the first claim on society's resources should be the guaranteeing of the best available standards and the widest area of choice to each member of society. A situation where the level of public provision was markedly lower than that available in the private sector to those who could afford it would be a denial of that socialist objective. Once that objective were achieved, however, individual decisions to purchase private provision, for whatever reason, could be viewed with equanimity.

In general, socialists should not be too zealous in looking for things to prohibit. In health and education, as in other fields, public provision does not necessarily inhibit choice – there is no reason why different forms of medicine and different types of schools should not flourish when funded by the public purse – but it remains true that private choice, as manifested through the private purse, is a useful guarantor of diversity and innovation. It should be challenged only when it threatens real damage to the interests of others in society; but we should be clear that when and if that challenge is made, it is made in order to protect and extend freedom, not to limit it.

The same approach will serve socialists well when it comes to the role of the market in a socialist society. There is an obvious tension between the operation of the market and the socialist concern for planning the most efficient and socially responsible use of resources. As we argued earlier, there is no reason why the market should not fulfil an important role in a socialist society – principally, as a more efficient and sensitive allocator of resources in the short term than could possibly be achieved by administrative diktat.

But the deficiencies of the market as a determinant of longer-term strategic issues mean that there must be a proper attempt to plan – something which, as the time-scale for major investment decisions lengthens and international competition in the efficient use of resources becomes more intense, is increasingly being recognised as necessary in most advanced societies but which can be done most effectively and sympathetically in a socialist society.

Oddly enough, the need for some degree of central planning – even if it means no more than the government of the day taking some responsibility for macro-economic policy – poses almost as great a problem for the socialist as it does for the *laissez-faire* capitalist. Although the socialist will welcome and demand planning as a necessary alternative to the capriciously short-term nature of market decisions, and as a means of ensuring that society meets its responsibilities to all its citizens, he will find that, potentially at any rate, it conflicts with another socialist objective – the maximum control for each individual over his own life.

In other words, the socialist objective at the level of the micro-economy will be to give each individual the maximum freedom of choice as an economic agent – as both consumer and producer. At the level of the macro-economy, however, the socialist planner may well wish to override the micro-economic decisions made by the individual or by co-operative enterprises in which the individual has a say (just as he would wish to override the micro-economic decisions made by the market).

The problem can be illustrated in terms of the savings which ordinary people make through institutions like pensions funds – savings which, by virtue of their massive size, have become a major element in the investment capital available to the British economy. At present, those savings are managed by professional managers whose responsibility under the law is to earn the best possible return on any investment they make.

The socialist might wish to say two things about these funds. First, he might say that, if the managers of the funds could be made properly accountable to the contributors, and if the law could be changed to allow for a wider range of objects than the simple maximisation of earnings, then a powerful agent of social ownership could be created. But secondly, he might also say that these huge sums offer an immensely important source of investment capital for longer-term projects which might be ignored by short-term market forces and that the macro-economic planner should be able to call on them in the national interest.

Both of these approaches are genuinely socialist; yet they seem mutually contradictory, in the sense that we cannot place such funds under the control of the contributors and at the same time hold them available for disposition by economic planners. Yet the conflict is more theoretical than practical. In the real world, there seems no reason why a workable compromise should not be reached between the interests of specific individuals and groups of individuals on the one hand and the objectives of economic planning on the other. This could be done either directly, by requiring, for example, a certain proportion of investment funds to be directed into particular purposes (something which is no more objectionable than taxation), or indirectly, by offering incentives, such as subsidised interest rates, to investments of particular types.

IS IT SOCIALISM?

Socialism in this form certainly avoids many of the pitfalls which beset those self-proclaimed socialist regimes which are so enthusiastically and gratefully attacked by socialism's critics; but can it be said to be truly socialist? Is it true to socialist traditions and values? Does it achieve socialism's objectives?

It must immediately be conceded that what is here advanced as socialism will seem gravely deficient to those who define their socialism in terms of Marxist doctrine. It is not so much that the end result, in practice, would be so very different from what they seek, but that there is little in the ideas here advanced of class struggle, inexorable economic laws, the dominance of the Party, and all those other hallmarks of scientific socialism. For those who like their political journeys to be well mapped out and signposted in advance, there is perhaps little here to suggest that they are in familiar territory.

Yet, for those who are prepared to look behind labels and slogans, and to look for principles and values, the approach argued for here is unmistakably socialist. It is, first, quite distinct from anything which a liberal or conservative or a social democrat might espouse. More importantly, it seeks to achieve the specifically socialist objectives of equality and social justice.

Nor is it entirely without support from other socialist writers, and particularly from those in the specifically British, non-Marxist tradition. It reflects the traditional preoccupations of British socialists with the ethical virtues of socialism, and with the need to seek support for measures of reform rather to organise for revolution. It pays due attention to the collectivism of British socialism but revives and gives greater prominence to that 'important tradition of socialist pluralism and participatory democracy' identified by Anthony Wright and principally associated with Cole and the Guild Socialists.

Laski, Tawney, MacDonald and Attlee all showed, in their writings, their interest in pluralism and in the notion that socialism was to be a liberator rather than a conqueror. Durbin stressed that democracy and socialism were inseparable, Strachey attacked excessive centralisation, while Crossman talked in terms of a socialism which diffused rather than encouraged the concentration of power. More recently, Raymond Williams has warned that even a socialist society 'degenerates into a system of privilege and exploitation unless it is policed by a social morality'.

The idea that socialism is about equality, the diffusion of

power and the liberation of the individual in society has, therefore, a long and undeniably socialist history. More importantly, it accords with the instincts and impulses of the great majority of those in Britain who are first attracted to socialist ideas; and it stands an excellent chance of securing the support of those who do not at present regard themselves as socialists – because they have, or are offered, a distorted perception of what socialism means – but who could be persuaded that socialism is what the rational person would demand, given the chance, as his condition for agreeing to enter society.

4 Equality

RAWLS – A NEW SOCIAL CONTRACT

We have so far established that there is a close connection between the maximisation of freedom and the achievement of a socialism whose main objective is the diffusion of power. They are linked by a common concern for achieving equality – an equality of freedom and an equality of power; and, for these purposes, freedom and power are very closely linked.

We now need to look in more detail at what we mean by equality and at its relationship with other concepts such as freedom and fairness. The supposed need to strike a balance between freedom and equality, the assumptions made about their compatibility or lack of it, and the consequences of these considerations for the concept of justice in society are at the heart of much political philosophy, and are of particular concern to the socialist. The socialist will wish to argue that justice, in the sense of a fair and universally acceptable distribution of basic social goods in society, is most nearly achieved through socialism.

These questions, however, go well beyond the concerns of socialists alone. In one of the most influential recent analyses of these issues, from a non-socialist viewpoint, John Rawls explored the relationship to each other of the concepts of freedom, equality and justice. His conclusions, though arguably not those which a socialist might have reached, are nevertheless an invaluable benchmark against which to evaluate socialist beliefs.

Rawls attempted, in *A Theory of Justice*, to construct a modern social contract – a hypothetical agreement – which would define the principles on which free and rational people might agree to enter society and arrange their affairs within society. The object of this exercise was to identify a working definition of justice, 'providing in the first instance a standard whereby the distributive aspects of the basic structure of society are to be assessed' (p. 9); in the course of it, Rawls pays particular attention to the relationship between freedom and equality and, in particular, to the circumstances in which people might be prepared to forego equality in return for other freely negotiated benefits.

It should be noted that, while Rawls is not or at least does not claim to be a socialist, he makes it clear that his analysis leaves open the question of whether or not a socialist society would be compatible with the principles which he claims would be voluntarily agreed by all people in society (pp. 274, 280). Our task is to press this question a litle further, and to ask whether the political implications of Rawls' hypothetical social contract, or of possible alternatives, are as ill-defined as Rawls suggests; or whether, on the contrary, the process which Rawls describes would not lead rationally and inevitably to a socialist organisation of society.

Many detailed criticisms have been made of Rawls' basic concept of the social contract. For our purposes, however, it is not necessary to pursue these questions. It is enough for us to note that Rawls' arguments have remained remarkably resistant to such criticism and to accept that his approach is more congenial both to the socialist approach and to the primacy of individual liberty as a social good than is the utilitarian doctrine to which he provides an alternative. His study provides us with an important tool with which to analyse some of the concepts which are central to the socialist position.

Rawls first asks us to imagine what he calls 'the original position'. In it, everyone about to enter into a social arrangement is assumed to operate from a starting point of equality behind a 'veil of ignorance' as to his place in society and the actual disposition of natural advantages – of intelligence, strength, and so on, and is then required, in conjunction with everyone else, to reach a free and rational agreement as to the principles he and they would regard as fair and acceptable for the society they are hypothetically about to enter.

Rawls does not of course suggest that such an operation was ever carried through. It is a purely hypothetical tool of analysis whose purpose is to identify those elements of social organisation which would enable us to say of a given society that it accords or not with our concept of justice or fairness.

Rawls argues that, in his hypothetical original situation, people operating behind the veil of ignorance would agree on two fundamental principles. First, he says, they would agree that everyone should have an equal right to the most extensive total system of equal basic liberties compatible with a similar system of liberty for everyone else. Secondly, they would agree that social and economic inequalities in society would be arranged and (by implication) justified only so far as they benefit everyone, particularly the least-advantaged (this is what Rawls calls the 'difference principle'), and are attached to offices and positions open to everyone under conditions of fair equality of opportunity.

The two principles would be placed, according to Rawls, in what he calls a lexical order – that is, the first principle would always take priority over the second, so that the second could take effect only to the extent that it was consistent with the first.

It is noteworthy that Rawls links two concepts in his first principle. He suggests that people would insist upon a right to freedom which is both equal with that of others, and which is also the most extensive liberty compatible with similar rights for others. In other words, people would give absolute priority to freedom above all other social objectives – the only limit to the total quantity of freedom available to the individual being the claims to equal liberty of other individuals – and would then give effect to the unique value they placed upon freedom by insisting that it should be distributed equally.

Assuming for the time being that there is no dispute about the meaning of freedom, Rawls' first principle is not dissimilar from – indeed, it is remarkably similar to – the concept of freedom which we advanced in an earlier chapter. He appears to accept that, so far from being incompatible, freedom and equality are closely linked and, by showing persuasively that a liberty which is equal and as extensive as possible is what free and rational people would insist upon, he provides an additional argument for that proposition. In accordance with the arguments advanced earlier, he would presumably agree that the most free society would be one which provides the highest possible degree of freedom enjoyed by the least free, or, in other words, one in which freedom is most equally distributed.

The unique value to be attributed to freedom is emphasised, too, in the fact that it receives different treatment in the first principle from that accorded to other social goods in the second principle, and in the priority which the first principle claims, by virtue of the lexical ordering, over the second principle.

So far, the socialist will find much in common with Rawls. It is when we come to consider the second principle that we run into problems. Those problems concern, first, the meaning and operation of the second principle itself, and, secondly, its relationship to the first principle.

RAWLS – INEQUALITY OF PRIMARY GOODS

The second principle, it will be recalled, provides that social and economic inequalities are to be arranged so that they are reasonably expected to benefit everyone, including the least advantaged, and so that they are attached to positions and offices open to all under conditions of fair equality of opportunity. The first puzzle is that the goal of equality, which played such a central part in the agreement embodied in the first principle, is downgraded so substantially in the second. If people in the original position were prepared to demand equality in respect of their freedom, why should they pay it so little attention when it comes to other social and economic factors (assuming for the moment that these have nothing to do with freedom)?

Equality in the second principle becomes merely a residual objective – a sort of default principle. If the conditions identified in the second principle are met, equality is displaced as a social goal by other considerations of utility and welfare. It is to come into play only if the conditions laid down are not met; but the whole thrust of Rawls' argument is directed towards the assumption that the conditions laid down in the second principle will be met. Rawls is remarkably reticent about how equality would work and what it would mean in the event that the conditions he prescribes were not met.

It is true that, to the extent that considerations of general welfare are to be modified by what Rawls calls the difference principle – the proposition that inequalities should benefit the least advantaged – and are to be governed by the condition of reasonable access, some concept of equality is imported into the second principle, but it is equality as a brake rather than a goal.

The goal of the second principle is the justification of inequalities, which are assumed to be inevitable, on the basis of the general and particular welfare which it is supposed they will promote.

This cavalier treatment of equality in the second principle is somewhat surprising. It is clear that the inequalities with which the second principle is concerned are not simply privileges to be enjoyed by some fortunate people in a social vacuum, since if this were the case, there would be no reason for other members of society to take them into account. The clear implication is that the inequality contemplated in the second principle is an equality enjoyed by some at the expense of others – that it is a question of unfair shares and of differential privileges which benefit some and disadvantage others. It is for this reason that it is to be tolerated only subject to certain conditions, such as that access to privilege should be reasonably open to everyone, so that, presumably, the unfairness can be justified on the basis of merit being rewarded.

The difference principle sits oddly in this context, since, by postulating that everyone should benefit from the permitted inequality, it seems to contradict the notion that the inequality in question is necessarily harmful. But if the inequality to be permitted by the difference principle does not prejudice some of those affected by it, why invent the difference principle to regulate it in the first place?

At the very least, the difference principle, therefore, seems to involve a paradox. It requires us to contemplate socially created inequalities which will, first, do harm to those who are disadvantaged by them, in the sense of depriving them of something they might otherwise have expected on the basis of equality and which they must give up in favour of others, but which will, secondly, confer on them additional benefits which outweigh the initial loss they suffer, at least in absolute and purely material terms.

The whole point of the difference principle is, of course, to permit and justify the receipt by some people of a greater than equal share of social benefits; and the permitted inequalities must, therefore, create benefits which are so substantial overall that they are even more valuable for the privileged than they are for the least advantaged. The inequalities must also create a disposition of benefits which is more advantageous to those who receive an unequally small share than would be provided by any other disposition, either on the basis of equality or of any other system of inequality.

There are immense problems in trying to decide whether a given set of social arrangements meets all these conditions. It may be said that these are hypothetical rather than practical questions; but unless it can be shown that some criteria and mechanisms exist for making judgments which are likely to be accepted by everyone in society, why should people in the original position bother with the difference principle in the first place?

The first problem is that a judgment as to whether or not the difference principle had been met might just about be made in a simplified model of society, where there were only two categories of people – the least advantaged and those who benefit from the inequalities. But what about a more complex society, more akin to real life, where there are many categories of people? What role is to be played by all those many people who find themselves in the middle echelons?

Rawls argues (p. 82) that the difference principle is met most completely at the point of maximum advantage to the least advantaged. But why should so little attention be paid to those only a little disadvantaged? Would an agreement by the most privileged to provide a specially advantageous deal for the least advantaged be enough to justify only the most minimal advantage for those only a little above them? And is the 'least advantaged' a single person, or a class of people, and if a class, how numerous must it be? Rawls concedes (p. 98) that these are difficult, if not insoluble, problems.

This gives rise to further problems. What happens if people were to disagree as to whether the permitted inequalities had in fact benefited everyone? Whose judgment on these matters is to prevail? Is it not likely that those whose power and freedom had been extended by the permitted inequalities would be able to use those advantages in an actual social situation to ensure that their views prevail? Is that not an outcome to be feared, with some justice, by all those in the original position?

There is also the problem that a given set of social arrangements might affect the distribution of what Rawls calls 'primary goods' – wealth and income, opportunities and powers, and so on – in a less than uniform way. Thus, certain social arrangements might increase income for some people, for example, but diminish their self-respect, which Rawls regards as the most important primary good. How is this situation to be evaluated? Again, Rawls appears to recognise the problem (p. 97) but he deals with it by merely assuming that 'primary social goods are sufficiently correlated . . . to avoid an index problem'. We shall have to return later to the relationship of self-respect to other social goods.

Even if it were agreed that the benefits promised by the permitted inequalities had materialised, would there not be a powerful temptation for those who turned out to get a less than equal share to require a periodic reckoning up, on the ground that it was their concession which had led to the production of those benefits and that they were entitled in return to obtain an equal share of the benefits which their concession had made possible? In other words, even on the most favourable assumptions about the benefits produced by inequality, would there not be a constant tension between the permitted inequality which produced the benefits and the demand for equality in distributing the proceeds?

Compliance or otherwise with the difference principle would have to be decided, in principle, by measuring an actual outcome, not against other practical situations, but against a virtually limitless number of other hypotheses. This dealing in hypotheses creates obvious difficulties in reaching any agreed assessment of the merits of a particular arrangement but it also gives rise to a further problem.

Why should those in the original position accept (at least to the extent of basing one of their two major principles upon it) in advance and without proof one hypothesis – the existence of inequalities which satisfy all the necessary conditions – when such an assumption depends on highly disputable arguments concerning the stimulus to growth and progress provided by the incentive of unfairly disproportionate rewards? Why should those who were eventually revealed to be disadvantaged have bothered with the hypothetical benefits which might arise from an inequality whose major consequence and purpose was in any case to provide greater benefits to other more advantaged people? At the very least, some assessment of the comparative advantages to be secured for everyone and for the least advantaged on the alternative hypotheses of inequality on the one hand and greater equality on the other would surely be required; yet this is what seems to be missing from Rawls' treatment.

This is despite the fact that the disadvantages of inequality – the loss of fair shares in the benefits of social co-operation – seem more certain and are logically prior to the more disputable benefits which might or might not accrue from tolerating inequality. The rational response of each individual to the possibility that he might prove to be disadvantaged when the veil of ignorance was lifted might be to negotiate some form of insurance provision against those obvious consequences of further inequality, so that those who proved to be less advantaged should be guaranteed at least a minimum benefit from the joint enterprise, to be calculated relatively to the benefits secured by others who were more advantaged.

Rawls deals with these points in a less than satisfactory way. He assumes, rather than argues or demonstrates, the benefits to be gained from inequality, and on the basis of that assumption, argues that people in the original position could have no rational reason for refusing to agree to the difference principle, since they could have nothing to lose by it. If the conditions specified by the difference principle were met, they would gain – at least in absolute and material terms, though some would lose comparatively and in terms of equality per se – and if the conditions were not met, then the difference principle would not apply and they would fall back on the principle of equality.

It is as though they were offered participation in a lottery, which might or might not be held; no entry fee is required and the only certain consequence, if they participate and if the lottery is actually held, is that prizes of varying sizes are won by each participant. Agreement to participate does not guarantee that the lottery will be held and indeed commonsense might lead one to doubt the likelihood of that happening; but the only element of risk, if the lottery is held, is that one participant might win less than others – so why not take part?

It is important to emphasise that this response by Rawls does not provide any support, as is sometimes argued or assumed, for the beneficent consequences of inequality. This is something which is simply not addressed by Rawls. All that he does is suggest a basis for ensuring that, if inequalities are to be permitted, they operate in such a way as to be generally acceptable. The possible advantages and the modes of operation of equality as a basis for his second principle are not explored.

Rawls treatment of this point does not, either, dispose of a further and more fundamental argument. Most people will surely feel that disadvantage in society is a relative rather than an absolute concept. They will feel more disadvantaged, even if in absolute terms their situation improves, when the gap between them and more advantaged people widens. This means that, for them, there is after all the possibility of losing out in the lottery, and the possibility will be realised if it turns out that they have won substantially less than others.

Rawls seems to pay too little attention to this point. He docs recognise that co-operating with others in society is a joint enterprise, and that the object of such co-operation, if achieved voluntarily, cannot be other than the production of benefits to be shared among the participants; but he seems insufficiently sensitive to the point that the cohesion of that joint enterprise and the continued willingness to participate will require attention to be paid, not so much to the absolute size of each share, as to the relation of each share to the others.

In society, all things are relative; the individual's standards are inevitably measured against those of others in society, not beyond it. His sense of well-being will be established in relation to the social goods possessed by others in his society. It will do little to comfort him, if he feels that he has fallen substantially behind his fellows, to be shown that on some absolute scale, which has little meaning to him within his society, he is better off than he would otherwise have been. Even if the question as to material benefits were answered in favour of inequality, in other words, those in the original position would surely be sensitive to the question of the non-material damage which might be done to social cohesion and to notions of fairness by ever-widening degrees of inequality.

Yet Rawls maintains that, once the difference principle begins to operate, equality per se no longer has any value. There is then no limit to the amount of additional advantage to be permitted to those already advantaged, and therefore no limit to the widening of the gap between favoured and less favoured. There are signs, though, that Rawls is himself uneasy about this; these can be detected in his treatment of the concepts of envy and of self-respect.

Thus, he seeks to downplay the sensitivity people might be expected to feel in respect of growing inequality by simply assuming, first, (p. 151) that those in the original position are not motivated by and will not recognise feelings of envy. He returns to the subject in more detail, however, when he discusses (pp. 530–41) the meaning of envy and its relationship to equality.

He defines envy as 'the propensity to view with hostility the greater good of others even though their being more fortunate does not detract from our advantages' (p. 532); the 'greater good' is to be measured according to an index of primary goods which, let it be noted, must include self-respect – 'the main primary good' (p. 534). Rawls explicitly links self-respect and envy (p. 534) when he says that 'a person's lesser position as measured by the index of primary goods may be so great as to wound his self-respect' and 'when envy is a reaction to a loss of self-respect in circumstances where it would be unreasonable to expect someone to feel differently, I shall say that it is excusable'.

Here, then, we have a clear statement from Rawls that a disparity in primary goods may both include and give rise to a loss of self-respect, sufficient to produce and excuse feelings of envy. Is this not an admission that equality per se has a value which those in the original position would be unlikely to ignore? Is there not a contradiction between saying that self-respect, as a primary good dealt with by the second principle, can with justice be distributed unequally, yet conceding that an inequality in (or wounding of) self-respect may give rise to excusable envy? And does this contradiction not threaten the whole viability of the second principle, since the 'excusable envy' arises from a loss of self-respect which is in turn the product of a 'lesser position' in terms of other primary goods – the very thing which the second principle is meant to make tolerable?

Rawls, however, baulks at this point. In proceeding to consider whether his difference principle would be likely to produce 'excusable general envy', he cites a number of reasons for supposing that it would not – that each person's self-respect would be bolstered by being treated, in the public domain at least, as an equal, that the painful visibility of gross disparities would be reduced by the greater ease of comparison with one's peer group rather than with the whole range of people in society, that the privileged would show self-restraint in showing off their advantages, and so on. Nowhere, however, does he appear to grapple with the central point – that a system which allows unlimited inequality seems bound to produce precisely the degree of disparity which will give rise to a loss of self-respect and, therefore, to envy.

A similar point can be made in respect of Rawls' treatment of the concept of self-respect. He concedes (p. 441) that self-respect is not an entirely self-regarding assessment, unaffected by any other social considerations, but is a social and relative concept – that it turns not only on one's opinion of oneself but also on the opinion one holds of others and on the opinion others have of oneself.

At times, he claims (p. 179) that his two principles will guarantee self-respect to each person, by publicly affirming men's respect for each other; but at others, he concedes, as we have seen, that self-respect will be destroyed by too great a disparity in primary goods. Thus, he seems to say that self-respect will be maximised by the equal distribution of rights and liberties under the first principle; but will be diminished, at least potentially, by an excessively unequal distribution of other primary goods permitted by the second principle. The only escape he appears to offer from this latter proposition is that he hopes people will not notice such an unequal distribution.

We are therefore entitled to ask how consistent Rawls is in his view of self-respect. How can it be both a corollary of equal liberty, as required by the first principle, but just one (though the pre-eminent) primary good, to be distributed according to the second principle, with its sanctioning of inequality? How can self-respect be one of those primary goods which will be made more plentifully available to everyone as a result of an unequal distribution, when it is at the same time threatened by the self-same unequal distribution of primary goods?

Most importantly, does Rawls or does he not believe that it is something to which people in the original position would have regard? There is no doubt that he attaches considerable importance to it, characterising it as 'the main primary good' and identifying it as one of the important and beneficial consequences of a proper application of his first principle. Why, then, does he not accept that, since his second principle permits the destruction of self-respect, there must be something wrong with that second principle, and that, on that ground, people in the original position would not accept it? Are there not times when Rawls comes close to saying, contrary to his own formulation of the difference principle, that self-respect can only be guaranteed by a distribution of both liberty and primary goods which is more equal than that permitted by the difference principle, and is this not a more acceptable formulation?

Rawls' problems in this regard seem to arise from a basic assumption he makes in the formulation of the difference principle – the assumption that additional social benefits depend uniquely on the efforts made by the naturally advantaged and that they will make those efforts only if provided with the incentive of a disproportionate share of the benefits. It is this assumption which makes it necessary to invent the difference principle, in order both to encourage the naturally advantaged to make those efforts and to ensure that the disproportionate reward they are assumed to be entitled to claim can be made acceptable to the less advantaged.

But this assumption is severely destructive of the self-respect of those who turn out to be naturally disadvantaged. They are required not only to accept, under Rawls' formulation, a 'lesser position' in respect of primary goods, but also to recognise that the increase in the quantity of such goods, from which they are permitted to benefit, was produced entirely through the talents and efforts of others.

A more reliable guarantor of the self-respect of each member of society would be a recognition that society is a joint enterprise in which the full exercise of individual talents, whether great or small, not only produces its own reward to the individual but is possible only within society; and that, as a consequence, the benefits of that joint enterprise, including of course the consequential social benefits arising from the exercise of individual talents, should be available as a matter of right to each member of society, by virtue of his agreement to participate.

The acceptance of this starting point would of course require the abandonment of Rawls' second principle. It would mean that people would approach the question of socially created benefits in much the same way as Rawls suggests they will treat the question of personal freedom – that is, they will agree that everyone should have an equal claim to such benefits. Only in this way can each person be assured that he will receive proper recognition of the contribution he makes by agreeing to participate in society; only in this way can he guarantee his self-respect and, arguably, his liberty. It is to this latter point that we now turn.

RAWLS – EQUALITY OF FREEDOM

In distinguishing between personal freedom and those matters of social, political and economic advantage or disadvantage which are the subject of the second principle, Rawls seems to accept Berlin's contention that freedom is different from what Berlin calls the conditions of freedom.

It will be recalled that Berlin dismisses arguments that these 'conditions of freedom' – matters of social and economic disadvantage – are deliberate constraints such as to affect and define the extent of individual freedom. They do no more than define, according to Berlin, the conditions in which a pre-existing freedom may or not be exercised.

Rawls seems to make a similar point when he says (p. 204) that:

> the inability to take advantage of one's rights and opportunities as a result of poverty or ignorance, and a lack of means generally, is sometimes counted among the constraints definitive of liberty. I shall not, however, say this, but rather I shall think of these things as affecting the worth of liberty . . .

This statement is open to the same objection as we made earlier to Berlin's distinction between freedom and the conditions of freedom. If the conditions of freedom affect the capacity to exercise it, and accordingly, (to use Rawls' terminology), its worth, then they must affect freedom itself, which has no meaning or worth unless it can be exercised. The constraints which define the 'conditions of freedom' and which determine its 'worth' must also define freedom itself.

Significantly, Rawls implicitly concedes the very point (about whether these constraints are deliberate) which Berlin contests. He does this by accepting the need to subject what are clearly socially created inequalities to very careful controls, on the implicit ground that without such controls they would prejudice some people in a way which would be unacceptable to them. He also seems to accept the proposition we advanced in an earlier chapter that there is a natural tendency in society towards inequality or the concentration of power.

This seems to be a clear admission by Rawls that the natural distribution of advantages can be re-ordered by social arrangements and that without deliberate countervailing measures those social arrangements are likely to prejudice at least some people by concentrating power in the hands of others. Rawls does not seem to have any doubt about the causal connection between these social arrangements and the disadvantage potentially suffered by some people, or about the possibility of changing, reducing or eliminating that disadvantage, and he therefore seems to concede what Berlin disputes – the human and coercive nature of these constraints.

This interpretation of Rawls' second principle is significant not only in the sense that it casts real doubt on Berlin's attempted distinction between the constraints which define freedom and what he calls the conditions of freedom; it also calls into question the second principle itself, and the distinction which Rawls draws between those matters affecting personal freedom on the one hand (dealt with by the first principle) and socially created inequalities (dealt with in the second principle) on the other.

In other words, if the inequalities dealt with in the second principle constrain, either potentially or actually, the social, economic and political areas of choice available to some people, and do so in a way that is clearly the consequence of certain social arrangements, why are they not relevant to the matters of personal freedom governed by the first principle? A person in the original position may not see the suggested distinction between the constraints on freedom, which are to be arranged so as to leave everyone with the maximum degree of equal liberty, and other constraints which are just as likely to limit his power of choice but which are to be arranged according to considerations of welfare rather than equality.

This point explains the unease which we feel about the fact that equality is given prime importance in the first principle but is downgraded substantially in the second. We suggested earlier that a rational person might be unwilling, on a variety of grounds, to forego equality as a goal in the second principle; and our difficulty in seeing the distinction between the subject matter of the first and second principles suggests another reason why this should be so.

A rational person in the original position would surely say that, when the veil of ignorance is lifted, his power of choice will prove to be limited by two separate sets of factors – the distribution of natural advantages and the socially created constraints – and that while there is nothing he can do about the first, he can ensure that the second operate as fairly, and therefore as equally, as possible. He will reject the contention that some of those socially created constraints will affect his freedom, and should be dealt with on the basis of equality, but that others (though prejudicing him in various ways) will somehow leave his power of choice unimpaired, and can therefore be allowed, provided only that they satisfy certain conditions about welfare.

He would therefore decide that only one principle was necessary – that social arrangements should produce the maximum possible area of freedom or power of choice for each person. He would point out that this required the most equal possible distribution of the advantages and disadvantages of social co-operation. He would insist on this, despite the inducements of possibly increased material benefits in return for greater inequality offered by Rawls, because he would see that increased inequality could only prejudice his freedom and his self-respect (which are clearly closely linked, in the sense of being responses to the same phenomena); and this, because his freedom is something to be defined in terms of his own social and economic powers, measured in relation to those exercised by others.

We are now in a position to sum up our objections to the formulation of Rawls' two principles. Although he tries hard to show that people in the original position will reach their decisions on purely rational grounds and will be completely free from value judgments, he allows at least two such value judgments to creep in – first, that inequality can be made acceptable because it is bound to produce additional advantages on such a scale as not only to benefit those who receive an unfairly small share of them but also to compensate them for their loss of comparability, and secondly, that the loss of comparability and the limitless widening of inequalities has no value in itself and is unlikely to matter either to the disadvantaged individuals or to society itself.

There can be no reason for anyone in the original position to make these assumptions or, therefore, to accept Rawls' second principle. Indeed, a rational concern for individual self-respect and for an equal and maximised freedom – based on the belief that freedom is something which must be capable of being exercised and that its exercise will be affected by inequalities – would require a quite different distribution of social goods from that which Rawls suggests.

EQUALITY AND SOCIALISM

Would the rational person in the original position who agreed with these criticisms of Rawls and who therefore insisted on an equal distribution of primary goods, including self-respect, be a socialist? We have seen that a socialist is one who wishes to ensure that the natural tendency in society towards the concentration of power is counteracted, by providing mechanisms for spreading and equalising power, and therefore freedom. In the sense that a social contract along the lines explained above would produce such an outcome, it can be characterised as embodying socialist principles. There are, however, two further points to be made concerning the socialist concept of equality.

The socialist would first of all agree with Rawls that there are or might be some inequalities, even those which are socially rather than naturally created, which he (or the hypothetical person in the original position) would be prepared to tolerate. The socialist would accept limited inequalities which were not prejudicial to others, since he would not regard them as affecting questions of power and freedom. He would distinguish between, for example, the accumulation of personal property for private enjoyment and the accumulation of private property as an instrument of economic power. The former he would regard as a non-prejudicial privilege, requiring no social regulation, until it reached such proportions as to deny to others that equality, including an equality of self-respect, which is the essential element of a free society.

Rawls himself makes a similar point (pp. 542–3) when he seeks to explain, as the justification for refusing to trade liberty against other social and economic goods, the diminishing marginal value, and therefore significance, of more and more material goods. This category of inequalities, acceptable on the ground that they did not matter, would not, however, be in any way the same as those which Rawls would tolerate because they satisfied his difference principle. All those inequalities which prejudiced some people, in the sense that they were denied a fair and equal share of the benefits of social co-operation, would be unacceptable to the socialist, even if they increased the general welfare or even the welfare of the least privileged.

The second point is that if those in the original position insisted, as we suggest they would, on extending the ambit of Rawls' first principle, so that freedom becomes a matter of inhibiting and removing certain sorts of inequalities, then it is important to be clear as to what might be meant by equality.

Equality could mean that the social arrangements agreed in the original position should take account of the naturally existing inequalities, and offset them by an unequal sharing of social benefits, so that the end result would be, as nearly as possible, that everyone had an equal amount of control over his own affairs and an equal capacity in relation to everyone else in society. The practical effect of this would be that someone naturally disadvantaged, let us say by being less intelligent than average, would be compensated by social arrangements which gave him a larger than average share of social benefits. This might be called the concept of equality of final outcome or what Rawls describes (p. 100) as the principle of redress.

It is sometimes suggested, usually by right-wing critics, that it is this concept of equality which is the goal of socialists. The modern socialist is, however, or ought to be, a realist. He is not concerned with any concept of total or final equality, because it is neither practicable nor desirable. The human condition varies infinitely from one individual to another. It would simply be impossible to ensure that everyone had an equal set of powers, talents and abilities, an equal capacity for enjoyment, and so on. Such an outcome would demand a form of personal engineering which would have to equalise temperaments and imaginations as well as minor matters like intelligence and aptitude for various activities – a form of engineering which is fortunately well beyond the state of any foreseeable art.

A society which gave overriding priority to the futile attempt to secure this impossible and undesirable objective would waste its efforts and prejudice the possible achievement of other objectives. Even if the objective of equality of final outcome could be achieved, thereby making possible the accomplishment of other social goals, this could be done only at the cost of an inequality in social benefit which would be just as inimical to individual freedom as the operation of a *laissez-faire* society.

This is because any attempt to achieve an equality of final outcome through providing a disproportionately large share of social benefits to the naturally disadvantaged would reduce the freedom of those whose share was reduced, since they would have to bear a greater degree of socially determined coercion (and therefore of limitations on their freedom) than they would have done if social benefits and constraints had been equally shared. In this case, the socialist would have to choose between maximising and equalising freedom on the one hand, and producing an equality of final outcome on the other.

It might be argued that there is an escape from this dilemma, if freedom is regarded as the area of choice left to the individual after taking both social and natural limitations into account. But this would be to ignore the fact that freedom is a social concept and can mean only the area of power of choice defined and limited by human or social coercion and constraints, rather than by natural (even though variable) limitations. To this extent, we must agree fully with Berlin. Provided that those humanly and socially applied constraints are applied equally, then the naturally determined and variable power of each individual to act within those constraints will not affect the question of his freedom, even if his natural power to act and do things within the area delimited by social constraints is greater or lesser than that of others.

Rawls makes it clear, of course, that redress or equality of final outcome is not his concern and that his second principle is in no way designed to achieve it. The second principle is much more concerned with a different concept of equality – what Rawls calls an equality of fair opportunity.

It is this concept which, it is often suggested, defines the goal of equality which the socialist should aim to achieve. In fact, although Rawls attempts to mitigate its full rigours by means of the difference principle, it is not a concept of equality at all, but rather, as the difference principle itself makes clear, an explanation and justification of inequality.

It provides few safeguards against a cumulative, damaging and ultimately unlimited increase in inequality. It masks and encourages precisely the sort of concentration of power and accumulation of advantage which the socialist is concerned to prevent. As we have seen, the guarantee of an absolute, as opposed to a relative, improvement in the position of the least advantaged cannot, and is not meant to, offset this impetus towards inequality.

It is this theory of inequality which seems to have been adopted as the central theme of the newly emerging Social Democrats. Based on what seems to be a partial mis-reading of Rawls – (Rawls does not assert or argue that inequality is beneficial but merely devises conditions on which it might be acceptable) – Owen adopts, in *A Future that Will Work*, a classic equality of opportunity position as an acceptable synthesis of liberal and socialist approaches.

It is ironic that, having attempted to adopt Tawney as a sort of philosophical godfather, the Social Democrats should have unerringly taken up a position which Tawney so scathingly labels as 'the Tadpole Philosophy' (*Equality*, pp. 108–9) – the doctrine that the fact that some survive and surmount social and economic inequalities is enough to show that those who fail to do so have no one but themselves to blame and that the system is essentially fair.

Tawney rightly castigates this blinkered view, describing equality of opportunity as likely to be illusory without 'equality of circumstances' (p. 111) and, in the absence of measures to prevent exploitation, as a mere jest. In making these points, Tawney was demanding a form of equality which took proper account of and reacted against the disparities in power which are certain to arise in society. As we shall see, this is much more like the approach which we shall argue that a socialist should adopt. It is therefore a little difficult for the Social Democrats to recruit Tawney to the cause of mere equality of opportunity.

If neither equality of final outcome nor equality of fair opportunity seems satisfactory as a socialist objective, what concept of equality should the socialist adopt? Should it not be something which is less impractical than equality of final outcome, but more far-reaching than the superficiality of equality of opportunity?

Equality for the socialist could and should mean the equal sharing of the benefits of social co-operation, so that that equal share was added to whatever share of natural advantages each individual was revealed to have when the veil of ignorance was raised. This might be called the concept of equality of social benefit; each person, as his condition for entering society, would insist upon a sort of social dividend which, because each person entered society on the same basis, would have to mean an equal share of the total benefits produced by social co-operation.

Those who turned out to be naturally advantaged might well contribute more to society than others; but they could not on that ground claim a larger than equal share of social benefits. The exercise of their natural talents would produce its own reward in terms of personal satisfaction; there could be no ground for claiming that their good fortune in terms of natural endowments should entitle them to additional social benefits as well.

An equal share of social benefit need not of course be the same for everyone. There would be a virtually unlimited range of forms which that equal share could take, and each person could, in principle, choose the form he preferred. As Tawney remarks (p. 39) 'Equality of provision is not identity of provision.' Equality need not inhibit, and should encourage, diversity.

In practical terms, an absolute equality of social benefit can, of course, never be achieved. But by setting itself this goal, and by constantly measuring social arrangements against it, a socialist society will provide itself with a motive power for equality and freedom which no other society can match.

What, however, of that other socialist objective of ensuring that the community takes responsibility for guaranteeing certain basic standards to everyone in society? Might that objective not require in some cases an unequal sharing of social benefits, in order to make good limitations, such as severe physical or mental handicap, imposed by natural factors?

Those in the original position would certainly wish to take account of the possibility that, when the veil of ignorance was removed, some of them might be revealed to fall substantially below the ordinary range of human abilities, and to need therefore the special care of others in society. The socialist, without wishing to overlook or discourage the personal virtues of compassion and generosity, would be unwilling to leave to their uncertain operation the fate of such very vulnerable people. He would therefore (and so, surely, would any rational person) insist that the first claim on society's resources must be adequate provision for such people – in absolute as well as relative terms.

In a very poor society, this prior claim on limited resources might mean that other principles agreed by those in the original position (such as equality) could not easily be implemented; a larger than equal share of social benefit might be needed, for example, to provide adequately for the severely handicapped. In modern Britain, however, the benefits of social co-operation are so great that their equal distribution will more than provide to everyone – even the most vulnerable – the fundamental requisites of a civilised life, in an absolute sense, sufficient to guarantee to everyone an equal degree of freedom from socially determined constraints. The modern socialist does not, therefore, have to choose between equality of freedom and adequacy of social provision; an equal share of social benefits will more than meet society's responsibility to its less advantaged members.

We can now conclude that the socialist would accept much of what Rawls argues. In particular, he would accept the usefulness of Rawls' basic concept, and the importance of equality as the basis for distributing freedom. He would part company with him, however, over the question of what falls within the first principle, and therefore of what is left to be dealt with in the second principle. The socialist believes that everything that matters, everything that affects the power relationships between people in society, must be dealt with in the first principle, since all socially determined factors which significantly affect power also affect freedom. Accordingly, only those social benefits which are, at least within certain limits, non-prejudicial and whose unequal distribution would not affect freedom fall within the second principle.

Since the socialist is indifferent to the question of how this limited category of benefits is distributed, he might be content to accept Rawls' difference principle, mainly on the grounds that, even if it did come into play, it would do so in an extremely limited area of no importance. It might be more accurate to say, however, that the socialist would see no need for any principle, other than the first principle, to regulate those factors which Rawls deals with under his second principle.

The rational person in Rawls' original position would surely take the socialist view. He would appreciate the dynamic nature of society and therefore the danger that an unequal distribution of social benefits such as would satisfy the difference principle might nevertheless lead to such a disparity and cumulative concentration of power as eventually to threaten the primacy of the principle of equal and maximum freedom. He would fear that the weaker people in society might be unable to ensure that full effect would be given to the first principle, when the dominant values and judgments in society would inevitably reflect the unequal power distribution sanctioned by the second. He would conclude that only an insistence on an equal distribution of power could guarantee justice and maximum freedom.

5 Conclusion

My constituency, in Dagenham, is a comparatively prosperous working class community. There is a little more space, and employment has been easier here, than in the decaying inner areas of our big cities. Many of my constituents live happy and fulfilled lives. But for many others, life is much less rewarding. It is a matter of few options, of subordination to dimly understood rules, of missing out on chances available to others, of a general feeling of powerlessness.

As householders, the majority are tenants of the local authority. The standard of the housing stock is generally good, but officials are having an increasingly difficult struggle, in the face of diminishing resources, to maintain the state of repair. The tenants find that, in order to get essential repairs done, they often have to engage in a long and wearying struggle with a hard-pressed officialdom.

If tenants should wish to move from one part of the borough to another or from one type of accommodation to another – by virtue of changes in their family circumstances or medical factors or any other reason – they again find that the options are limited. The pressure of demand on the number of housing units available – especially family houses – is too great to allow for easy movement; to obtain a transfer means an often lengthy and difficult process of committee meetings and formal decisions which, by their very nature, cannot always be perfectly sensitive to individual circumstances.

Tenants are often restricted in innumerable other ways. They have little choice as to how their accommodation should be arranged and decorated; if they do obtain permission to install their own fittings – even if they represent some real improvement in comfort or convenience – they will be obliged to have them removed at their own expense when they vacate the tenancy. They have only limited rights to pass on the tenancy to members of their families. They are often bewildered and disheartened by the dirty and vandalised environment in which they live.

For those in work, the greater part of their working lives is spent under the direction of a boss or foreman. Work is drudgery – a whole chunk of living handed over to someone else – a someone else who is often impersonal and remote, and at times unreasoning. For most, there is little choice of employment. The unemployment rate has risen to 12 per cent, and those in work are glad to have jobs and aware of the limited opportunities for those out of work. Both the local authority and manufacturing industry – for long the major employers – now provide fewer job opportunities. There is a strong sense, especially among the young, that society no longer needs them.

Most workers belong to trade unions. For a disturbingly large number, however, the trade union is almost as remote an institution as the distant boardroom in which their management make decisions. The level of wage claims, decisions to take industrial action, the formulation of national union policy, often seem to be matters dealt with by powerful people who are in no sense under the control of the membership. Often, the mechanisms for participation exist, but are not taken up. It is a moot point as to whether it is apathy which produces the alienation or the other way round.

The options are even more limited for those out of work – not just the unemployed, but all those who, for one reason or another, look to the state for support. About half of my constituents now receive some form of means-tested benefit. Their living standards, their day-to-day spending, the very pattern of their lives, turn on rules and decisions which they only vaguely understand. They often feel humiliated by having to claim what some still see as charity. When the new housing benefit scheme was introduced without adequate preparation, there were many cases, especially among the elderly, of people being frightened and shamed by threats of eviction on account of arrears which had arisen, without their knowledge or responsibility, but through administrative confusion.

It is easy for people who feel themselves to be so much at the mercy of 'the system' in respect of their employment, their living conditions and their purchasing power to feel similarly powerless in respect of other manifestations of authority – the police, the medics, the schoolteachers. They have been conditioned to think of themselves as not counting for much; they feel themselves at a disadvantage in dealing with people who are more powerful, and perhaps better educated and more articulate. As a result, they get less from the services provided than they might.

The services themselves are often deficient, at least by comparison with those provided elsewhere. The hospitals are less well equipped and staffed. In the field of education, the recruitment of good teachers is a problem. There is a feeling that higher education is 'not for the likes of us'. My constituents are less well protected, less well educated, less well cared for in health matters, less well served in general by public authorities.

On the rare occasions when they feel aggrieved enough to want to identify and enforce their rights – against employer, or neighbour, or public authority – they are generally uncertain as to how to proceed. Recourse to law, in particular, is for them a long, confusing and expensive business, which only very rarely produces satisfactory results.

For an unskilled man without a job but with a family, dependent on means-tested benefits to make ends meet, worried about his wife who is depressive, unable to afford the heating needed to remedy the dampness in his sick child's bedroom, there are not many choices. He cannot find a job, he cannot move or improve his accommodation, his expenditure is strictly limited and determined for months in advance by the benefit rates laid down in the regulations. It is hard for him to see how he can escape from these constraints; he has neither the qualifications nor the self-confidence to break out.

By any absolute standard, he is not badly off. But as a member of this particular society, he is substantially disadvantaged; the social and economic constraints to which he is subjected severely limit his freedom of choice by comparison with others in society. In particular, it would not be surprising if his self-respect – which Rawls identifies as the most important primary good and which should therefore never be diminished by social arrangements – should reflect the powerless position in which he is put by society.

It may be objected that this picture is an exaggerated one, which not even those depicted in it would recognise. It is certainly true that the deficiencies I mention do not often all occur together and that they are in any case often offset by other factors; people are very often able to rise above or circumvent constraints of this type by deriving rich satisfaction from family life, or from the exercise of personal talents and the pursuit of personal interests. Yet it remains the case that, for a substantial minority, life is made poorer and less rewarding by some or all of the factors I mention.

What is the relevance to this of questions of socialism and freedom? Can it really be argued that people are less free as a result of these factors, and that socialism will help to liberate them?

It should be said straightaway that, in terms of civil and political rights, my constituents are all as free as can reasonably be expected in a modern society. They have the vote, a substantial measure of freedom of speech and of political thought and action; they have the more or less even-handed protection of the law.

Nor are these freedoms regarded by them as unimportant and illusory. While membership of political parties or pressure groups is small, and the turn-out in local elections is low, three-quarters of those eligible to vote in general elections do so. Anything perceived as a serious interference with these fundamental rights would be fiercely resisted.

Yet, for the reasons set out in the second and fourth chapters, the social and economic factors which hem them in and which limit their choices and freedom of action must be reckoned to make them less free, at least by comparison with those who have much more extensive social and economic power in society. Because of the way in which we are accustomed to looking at these issues, we do not normally describe these limitations in terms of freedom; we should be more inclined, if required to think about them and to categorise them at all, to say that they involved questions of power, wealth and status. But they do affect freedom; and the question must then arise as to how that freedom is to be enlarged.

We have already established that, unlike the more familiar civil and political liberties, freedom in the social and economic sphere is not a matter of absolutes. It cannot be established by providing powers and entitlements defined without reference to the powers and entitlements enjoyed by others in society. It is essentially a relative concept; freedom in this sense is threatened as the gap in social and economic power between some people in society and others widens, and it is strengthened as that gap diminishes.

This means that no doctrine which encourages or permits, palliates or justifies, an unlimited or even a substantial inequality in fundamental social and economic powers can be regarded as compatible with the highest possible degree of individual liberty. Those who wish to extend the freedom of each individual in society are surely bound to embrace a doctrine whose objective is, so far as is practicable, the equalisation of social and economic powers. That objective, as we argued in the third chapter, is the essential element of socialism.

Why, then, do my constituents not (in general) regard socialism as the path to their salvation and themselves as socialists? They have for several generations voted Labour in large, though diminishing, numbers; but that is by no means the same thing as embracing socialism. They vote Labour, so far as one can tell, because of a residual loyalty to Labour as 'their' Party. This is especially true of older people. That loyalty has remained, despite some disillusion with the Labour Party arising from Labour's performance in government and from a cynicism with regard to politics generally; but loyalty is by its very nature a diminishing asset. The Labour Party has generally failed to make any real appeal to a new generation of electors.

Most Labour voters, if asked to define socialism, would probably do so in terms of nationalisation, bureaucracy, trade unions and even welfare state scroungers – all phenomena which opinion polls and personal observation tell us are unpopular, even with Labour voters. And if persuaded to think about the compatibility of individual freedom and socialism, they might agree with the promptings of those who suggest that socialism would inevitably mean less liberty.

They probably accept that a socialist government would genuinely try to improve the material conditions and comparative position in society of working people; but they would not see this as obviously relevant to freedom. And, whatever they thought of that objective, many Labour voters might express doubts as to whether their more familiar civil and political freedoms would remain intact in a socialist regime. Many would be likely to identify the state and local government bureaucracies as the major constraints on their liberty, and to overlook or be unaware of the less obvious constraints imposed by the economic and social system.

This is, if right, no more than a predictable consequence of the very great propaganda efforts made by the opponents of socialism and of the insidious conditioning to which we are all subject by virtue of living in a society which elevates its own prevailing values to the status of universal truths. But it is partly, too, a reflection of the image of socialism which socialists themselves have fostered.

The voters have constantly before them the model of supposedly socialist regimes whose suppression of individual liberties is uncontested and well-known; if they do not themselves draw the obvious conclusions, there are plenty of eager propagandists to help them do so. As British socialists, we have only ourselves to blame if we insist on promoting a version of socialism which emphasises, in its ambitions at any rate, its similarities with these repressive regimes, and which therefore forfeits the popular support which is both an essential element of socialism in a mature democracy and the necessary condition of its implementation.

The socialism we offer is long on dogma and jargon, and short on commonsense and realism; it is strong on sectional interest and talk of class war and weak on the virtues of equality and co-operation; it emphasises restriction and compulsion and pays little attention to the enlargement of choice and the liberation of the individual; it affects at times to downgrade parliamentary government and the rule of law as bourgeois preoccupations and to elevate the Party (and particularly the activist) as the pre-eminent force in society. There is little prospect of success in Britain for a socialism conceived of and presented in this way.

It need not be like this. We can offer a socialism which is at the same time truer to the socialist ideal and more likely to attract popular support; and, far from shirking the problem of individual freedom, we should welcome it as being the ground on which our arguments are seen at their strongest.

We must emphasise that the true concern of the socialist is *the individual* in society – every individual, and not just the members of some élite, whether identified by wealth or social status or Party membership or any other criterion. This concern for each individual means that the socialist cannot tolerate a society in which the interests of only some individuals prevail, to the exclusion or devaluation of the interests of others. To the socialist, society is a co-operative enterprise in which the fact of participation is enough to provide an entitlement to equal respect and an equal share of social benefits.

This means, as we have constantly emphasised, that a socialist society would be one in which the institutions and rules were arranged so as to prevent concentrations of power from arising and to counteract and break them down when they did arise. This would require constant vigilance against the pretensions of capitalists, bureaucrats, Party apparatchiks, collectives and the like. It would mean not only an attack on the inequalities produced by the current dominance of capital and property, but an attack, too, on the concentrations of power permitted and encouraged by government bodies and trade unions. It means that we must also defend and extend those aspects of our present society which protect the individual – most importantly, those rules and institutions which establish his civil and political rights.

In its concern for each individual, and in its resistance to concentrations of power, a socialist society would necessarily promote the interests of those who are currently disadvantaged; but socialism is not a class-based doctrine. It need not and should not talk the language of class war; its triumph is not that of a particular class but the achievement of the greatest possible degree of equality and of control for each individual over his own life.

The pursuit of equality has traditionally been seen as conflicting with the maximisation of individual liberty. It is for this reason that socialists have usually fought shy of engaging their political opponents on this battle ground. But, following the arguments presented here, we can assert that the diffusion and equalisation of power – the true business of socialism – is not only the path to social justice (in the Rawlsian sense) but is also the only way to achieve a truly free society in which each individual enjoys the maximum degree of freedom commensurate with a similar degree of freedom for all others. We can go further; we can say that the social goals of equality, justice and freedom are not only compatible but can only be achieved together, and that socialism is the only means by which that can be done.

Socialism in this country has been inhibited by a failure to secure popular support for and understanding of the aims of a socialist society. That failure has in turn reflected another deficiency – a lack of clarity and conviction on the part of those who have propagated socialist principles. What has weakened and destroyed the impulse towards socialist reform has been a lack of intellectual confidence.

Those who advocate a substantial re-arrangement of a given social order can always be sure of powerful opposition from entrenched interests. Every attempt will be made to undermine them. It is the erosion of confidence, rather than deliberate betrayal, which has so often led to the faltering of Labour politicians in government. It is our vulnerability to the attacks of our opponents which has created the uncertain and unattractive image which we now present to the electorate. Only the most secure foundations – intellectual and moral – can withstand such pressure and enable us to re-build that popular support we need, and which alone will produce an irresistible demand for a just, free and socialist society.

Index